Flexischooling
England and Wales
Edition 1

By

Peter Humphreys

With Contributions from

Alison Sauer and Emma Dyke

The Centre for Personalised Education

Published by

Educational Heretics Press

Originally published in Kindle Format 2018 by **Educational Heretics Press**[i] in conjunction with **The Centre for Personalised Education.**[ii]

Published in Paperback by Educational Heretics Press in 2019

Educational Heretics Press, 7 Cardington Drive, Shrewsbury, Shropshire, SY1 3HD

Peter Humphreys, Alison Sauer and Emma Dyke have exercised their right to be identified as authors under the Copyright, Design and Patent Act, 1998.

© Peter Humphreys, Alison Sauer, Emma Dyke

Title: Flexischooling Guidebook: England and Wales Edition 1

ISBN: 978-1-900219-56-3

Editor: Bryony Cooper-Brown

Design and Production: Educational Heretics Press

Cover design: by Mike Wood (EHP)

Cover Image by: ID 47303422© Embe2006 Dreamstime.com

British Cataloguing in Publication Data – A CIP record may be obtained from the British Library

Contents

Introduction

This book serves as a practical reference for any family considering flexischooling. It also supports schools, local authorities, researchers, media and interested citizens in finding out more about the concept. As chapters are addressed to specific audiences there is intentional repetition of some content. It offers salient flexischooling information and links.

Further information can be found on the Centre for Personalised Education's website, social media (detailed below) and, in due course in hard copy publications.

Other information and support can be found here:

- Centre for Personalised Education - website[iii]
- CPE - Flexischooling Families UK -Facebook[iv]
- CPE - Flexischooling Practitioners UK -Facebook[v]
- Centre for Personalised Education -Facebook[vi]
- Home Education and your Local Authority: Help with dealing with officialdom[vii]
- Centre for Personalised Education -Personalised Education Now (Twitter)[viii]
- Centre for Personalised Education – Facebook Page[ix]
- Hollinsclough CE Primary Academy[x]
- Hollinsclough Flexischool Federation[xi]
- Educational Heretics Press - website[xii]
- Educational Heretics Press -Facebook Page[xiii]
- CPE - Light on Ed Research Network - Facebook[xiv]
- CPE - Legal Advice for Educational Start-ups - Facebook[xv]

Chapter 1. Flexischooling Overview

1.1 What is Flexischooling?

The information here applies to flexischooling as it currently exists in England and Wales.

Flexischooling is an arrangement where a learner is registered at school and has a full-time education but is educated partly in a school setting (primary or secondary) and partly elsewhere (commonly home-based). It can be a long or short-term arrangement. Flexischooling is a local agreement between the school (head teacher) and families. It is a legal option but, there is no right to flexischool. This is at the discretion of the school (head teacher). The legal framework can be found in Chapter 4 and at:

http://www.personalisededucationnow.org.uk/law-and-guidance/[xvi].

Flexischooling 5-19.

There are examples of flexischooling across the age-range and in a variety of diverse settings. In some, there will be just one or two children flexischooling, in others, flexischoolers will be in greater numbers up to and including those where the majority of pupils are flexischooled. Such settings can justifiably be labelled as a flexischool.

Part-time schooling pre-compulsory school age.

Flexischooling is not to be conflated with part-time schooling prior to compulsory school age. This is a parental right and must be accommodated by schools (see Admissions Code (Dec 2014)[xvii] Section 2.16). See also our briefing sheet Part-Time Schooling in England (Under5)[xviii] reproduced in Chapter 4.

Funding.

Learners are registered as full-time with the school and as such are fully-funded. Schools have the budgetary resource to ensure flexischooling can work effectively.

The Flexischooling Continuum.

Flexischooling sits along a continuum. At its simplest it is a basic flexitime arrangement where the school-based and home-based learning are discrete. The mainstream education system has traditionally accommodated this to some extent with nursery and early years' provision. There are also examples of some secondary schools who offer flexitime contracts to students who earn the right to study away from school for periods.

So, even at this end of the continuum, flexischooling begins to question some basic assumptions about schooling, accepting:

- a single location is not essential
- parents can have an active role
- children / young people can learn without teachers being present
- facilitating learning is as much part of teaching as formal instruction
- resources at home/elsewhere both physical and virtual can be utilised
- uniqueness of individuals / individual learning

dispositions can be respected and accommodated

At the more transformational end of the spectrum, flexischooling can go further in confronting notions about schooling and traditional views of learning. This type of flexischooling recognises the rapidly changing world, the ubiquitous availability and ease of knowledge access, and the complexities of life and behaviour. It recognises that flexible people develop a wider range of coping strategies and are better equipped for life in the modern world and workplace. Flexibility in all dimensions is then the key.

1.2 Why Flexischool?

Parents

There are many reasons why parents choose flexischooling, such as:

- Parents wish to spend more quality time with their children. They want an active role in their children's education.
- Children can follow their own interests, and different learning styles can be respected and accommodated.
- Children can benefit from both approaches to learning; being taught at school and being educated at home.
  - At school children can work and socialise with their own peer group, they have access to specialist educators and resources they might not have at home, they can join in with activities such as school trips and plays.
  - At home children can benefit from individual tuition or small, possibly mixed age, groups,

alternatively their learning can be self-directed, and they can experience a wider range of activities in different environments, e.g. outdoor activities, museum visits.

- Children who have difficulties attending school full-time, for example because of illness or emotional or behavioural needs, have the opportunity to follow a reduced timetable without being removed from the school environment altogether.

Flexischooling offers educational journeys and experiences more fitting for the 21st Century. There is space to accommodate self-direction and co-creation and an altogether more personalised approach in contrast to the wholly more prescribed, one size fits all structures and progressions in full-time schooling.

School and Local Authorities

The benefits of flexischooling are not confined to parents and learners. Schools and local authorities can reap huge rewards in terms of working creatively in ways more closely reflecting the needs of pupils, families and communities. Schools and local authorities consistently struggle to meet statutory educational duties, let alone moral and social imperatives to learners and families. The pressures of rigid curricular progressions, timetables, assessments and lack of resources particularly in times of austerity, can render full-time schooling a miserable experience for many children. The potentially life-damaging consequences are only too real and costly to society. Flexischooling is a way to respond to these challenges with transformational pragmatism.

Additionally, some schools are threatened with closure because they are undersubscribed. Small schools in rural areas often fit this criterion. Flexischooling has proven to be a practical solution in changing the fortunes of these schools and the communities they serve, by putting them on a sustainable footing. Furthermore, such schools have begun to look more innovatively at what they offer and how they do it. Flexischooling has the potential to benefit children, families, the wider community, individual schools and even the education system as a whole.

Society at large

Our society is quite rightly concerned with issues like education, equalities, safeguarding, democracy and cohesion. Therefore, it is utterly frustrating that the schooling system scores so many 'own goals' for learners with its rigidity and inability to facilitate a personalised education. The unintended consequences for children can include; damage to mental and physical health, poor learning, thwarted aspirations and failure to fulfil potential.

The current school system is counterproductive. It fundamentally denies young people self-expression, control over their own bodies, lives and learning. The results are evident in the dependency and reward-oriented behaviours of modern learners. The products of this system are becoming increasingly characterised by their lack of independence, innovation, creativity, deep engagement, cooperative and group working skills. This all runs counter to the kinds of people we need in the 21st century and, critically, to the healthy, resilient, creative and committed citizens our societies need to thrive. Flexischooling can begin to redress these problems and perhaps point towards how mainstream learning systems can transform into something more effective and appropriate.

In summary, although many parents may come to flexischooling out of desperation and frustration with the impact of full-time schooling on their children and the family as a whole, others will come out of a conviction that flexible educational journeys and experiences are more desirable in the education of the whole person and are more aligned with the world we live in. All flexischooling parents, however, seek a more effective and efficient educational model. Experience also shows that schools are more prepared to look creatively at their educational offer and this dynamic holds potential for the whole schooling system.

Flexischooling is not, and probably will never be, suitable for all families and all circumstances. However, for a significant number it is a game changer. What flexischoolers bring to the development of our learning system are lessons about the paucity of our current system and the ultimate denial of control over the direction of our own lives, creeping authoritarianism and lack of democracy.

Far from being an odd group at the margins, flexischooling families and flexischools are trailblazers. They deserve to be listened to, learned from and worked with.

Chapter 2. Current Reality

Flexischooling has a long, successful and honourable history.

It is beneficial to children, parents, schools, communities and the country at large. Elsewhere in the world, for example British Columbia, it is considered to be a credible option as valid as full-time school attendance.

As advocates of flexischooling, we at The Centre for Personalised Education recognise that administrative arrangements require much greater clarity. The school attendance codes, attendance procedures, safeguarding advice and so on were not designed with flexischooling in mind. Therefore, schools have needed to take best-fit decisions in the context of often contradictory, vague or inappropriate advice from government departments and local authorities.

Although flexischooling is in its infancy, its positive impact on learners and families alone is sufficient reason for it to be taken seriously and made more widely known as a credible and viable option. The impact is also felt in schools and some schools like Hollinsclough CE Primary Academy are already pushing at boundaries and exploring the potential scope of flexischooling

It's not hard to see how we have arrived at the current position. The law has tolerated flexischooling, yet there has been no active promotion or accommodation of it. It appears that successive governments have been unaware of the extent of flexischooling and not considered there was sufficient need to provide parents, local authorities or schools with adequate information and guidance. The guidance and legislation[xix] that exists is sparse, unsatisfactorily developed and inflexible in practice. Furthermore, at the time of writing, the government appears to be actively discouraging flexischooling by giving schools advice that misinterprets the law. They have even removed section 5.6 of the Elective Home Education Guidelines 2007[xx] which obliged local authorities to 'make sure that head teachers are made familiar with flexischooling and how it may work in practice.'

Flexischooling has always been a local agreement negotiated by families, head teachers and governors. Parents who pursue flexischooling have had to be determined and committed as local authorities, schools, teachers, parents and students are often unaware of, and resistant to, the practice or indeed any alternatives to full-time schooling. In addition, the reputation of flexischooling is distorted by unhelpful stereotypes, inaccuracies and disinformation. It's unlikely to be found in university-based initial teacher education or school-based teacher training pathways.

At local authority level, officers with a background in education were traditionally employed to oversee elective home education, education other than at school, and flexischooling. These officers typically had good educational knowledge and strong relationships with alternative education providers and were often ex-teachers. Sadly, cutbacks and a growing emphasis on numbers rather than pedagogy have led to these staff being replaced by those with a background in education welfare or attendance. In turn, this has led to a less sympathetic approach toward flexischooling and other alternatives to traditional full-time schooling. According to Wendy Charles Warner, in her research *Home Education and the Safeguarding Myth: Analysing the Facts behind the Rhetoric*, children who are educated outside of school are subject to disproportionate scrutiny from agencies who wrongly believe them to be at an increased risk of harm. Local authority children's services departments focus on these imagined safeguarding issues along with excessive concern for school attendance statistics rather than tangible educational outcomes. This research is available at

There is clearly a problem here. We would argue that more needs to be done to raise the positive profile of flexischooling and to address the information vacuum and inconsistency of messages.

The most obvious consideration now is to look comprehensively at flexischooling and how it can be accommodated within appropriate legal, funding, registration and guideline structures. This will necessitate a pause and consultation with those involved. The Centre for Personalised Education's advocacy of flexischooling works at all levels; supporting parents, families, learners and schools. We engage with local authorities and government departments. It would be advantageous to secure a cross-party understanding of the place and contributions of flexischooling to the educational landscape. Once established the bureaucratic and administrative procedures and safeguards can be put in place and regular sensible review scheduled.

Chapter 3. Legal Framework

What follows is our latest flexischooling information sheet on the legal framework. It can also be downloaded here: **Is Flexischooling Legal in England?**[xxi]

Is Flexischooling Legal in England?

The simple answer is yes, although lots of people, including teachers, parents and school governors, believe that it isn't.

What is flexischooling?

Flexischooling is an arrangement whereby children of compulsory school age receive their education partially at school, and partially elsewhere under the supervision of their parents.

Is it the same as part time education?

No, part time education is only allowed in law as a temporary solution to a specific problem, usually for medical or mental health reasons or for integrating a pupil into a new situation.

Flexischooling is different. Flexischooling provides children with a full-time education although not all of it will occur in school. It can be a temporary or permanent arrangement and may be requested for a wide variety of reasons.

Under what circumstances is flexischooling allowed?

Schools may agree to parental applications for flexischooling regardless of the qualifications of the parents or their reasons for choosing flexischooling. Legally flexischooling can commence when a private arrangement is reached between the school and the parent which fulfils the attendance register requirements of The Education (Pupil Registration) (England) Regulations 2006 regulation 6, and when the school is satisfied that the child will receive a suitable, full time education overall.

The Education (Pupil Registration) (England) Regulations 2006 regulation 6(4))

(4) An approved educational activity is either—

- (a) An activity which takes place outside the school premises and which is—

- (i) Approved by a person authorised in that behalf by the proprietor of the school;

- (ii) Of an educational nature, including work experience under section 560 of the Education Act 1996(1) and a sporting activity; and

- (iii) Supervised by a person authorised in that behalf by the proprietor or the head teacher of the school; or

- (b) Attendance at another school at which the pupil is a registered pupil.

Will flexischooling affect the school's funding?

No, because the funding is currently applied to a place at a school not the number of hours the child attends. Therefore, schools currently receive the same funding for flexischooled pupils as they would for a child receiving all of his/her education in school.

What if the child has special educational needs?

Flexischooling is a legal and viable option for all children regardless of SEN, even if the child has an EHC plan or SEN statement, or attends a special school. Sometimes flexischooling is written into the plan as the appropriate provision for the child.

Does the National Curriculum Apply?

Yes, to the school-based part but not necessarily the non-school based part. In law, the national curriculum does not apply to the non-school based part of the education of a flexischooled child unless this was part of the arrangement/agreement between the school and the parent.

What about SATs?

SATs are a statutory requirement for schools, so the normal rules apply, and the child will be expected to sit them all.

How does Ofsted view flexischooling?

To the best of our knowledge no school has been marked down for allowing flexischooling. The schools we are aware of that have the majority of the children on roll subject to a flexischooling arrangement have been praised for their provision and meeting of the children's individual needs.

What about safeguarding?

Safeguarding is the responsibility of the parents or of any person acting in loco parentis. Essentially, whilst the child is at school the school is responsible for safeguarding. At all other times the parent is responsible unless the child is being cared for/educated by somebody else. For example, if a child is at a swimming lesson the swimming pool staff are responsible for safeguarding. The school cannot legally be held responsible for the welfare of the child in the part of the school day where the child is by agreement not in school.

How is flexischooling recorded in the register?

There are currently two options:

Where the child is part time educated at school and part time electively home educated (i.e., with neither oversight nor approval from the school) then the registration mark used is "C" - authorised absence – for the non-school sessions. Naturally this affects the attendance figures of the school, which can be problematic, but Ofsted takes the stance that so long as the pupils are educated that is what is important.

Where the arrangements meet the criteria for "Off-site educational activity" (see The Education (Pupil Registration) (England) Regulations 2006 regulation 6(4)) then a "B" code can be used which does not affect attendance figures.

Code B: Off-site educational activity

This code should be used when pupils are present at an off-site educational activity that has been approved by the school. Ultimately schools are responsible for the safeguarding and welfare of pupils educated off-site. Therefore, by using code B, schools are certifying that the education is supervised, and measures have been taken to safeguard pupils. This code should not be used for any unsupervised educational activity or where a pupil is at home doing school work. Schools should ensure that they have in place arrangements whereby the provider of the alternative activity notifies the school of any absences by individual pupils. The school should record the pupil's absence using the relevant absence code.

In order to meet these criteria, the school must authorise the parent to provide the education, and possibly also approve the education that will be taking place. This authorisation and approval may be granted on a termly or annual basis through a meeting or exchange of reports between the school and the parent.

In summary, if the school have authorised the parents to manage the education taking place in the session or have approved the education planned to take place then "B" can be used, otherwise a "C" must be used.

Centre for Personalised Education, April 2017.

Chapters 4-7

The following chapters will focus specifically on the needs and perspective of different audiences – Parents, Schools, Learners and Local authorities. In them we will unpack, develop and cross reference the previous information.

Chapter 4. Information and Guidance for Parents

What follows is our latest flexischooling information sheet for Parents. It can also be downloaded here: [xxii]

4.1 Parent's Leaflet (over 5 only)

What is flexischooling?

Flexischooling is an arrangement whereby children of compulsory school age receive their education partially at school, and partially elsewhere under the supervision of their parents.

Flexischooling is a perfectly legal option, but there is no guaranteed right for parents to flexischool. Whilst they may request that their child is flexischooled it is entirely at the discretion of the Head teacher. The education provided at home and at school must together constitute a full-time provision.

Why do parents choose flexischooling?

There are many reasons why parents choose flexischooling, such as:

- Parents wish to spend more quality time with their children

- They want an active role in their children's education

- Children can follow their own interests

- Different styles of learning can be respected and accommodated

- Children can benefit from both worlds; being taught at school and being educated at home

- Children who have difficulties attending school full-time, for example because of illness or emotional or behavioural needs, have the opportunity reduce the amount of time spent in school whilst still receiving a full-time education.

At school children can work and socialise with their own peer group, they have access to specialist educators and resources they might not have at home, they can join in with activities such as school trips and plays.

At home children can benefit from individual tuition or small (mixed age) groups, their learning can be self-directed, they can experience a wider range of activities in different environments, e.g. outdoor activities, museums visits

How does flexischooling work?

The Flexischooling Agreement.

When a parent is interested in making a request for a flexischooling arrangement, contact must be made directly with the Head teacher of the school so that the proposal may be considered.

Once the decision to flexischool is made parents and head teacher should meet and discuss how the arrangement will work. Following this discussion, a written and signed agreement is formulated between the school and parent in order to make expectations clear for all concerned. The agreement should include:

- The expected pattern of attendance at school.

- What areas of education each party will provide?

- To what extent the National Curriculum will be followed in the non-school based element of flexischooling.

- How school and parents will co-operate to make flexischooling work, e.g. regular planning meetings between parent and school to ensure the child achieves his or her potential and to promote good home-school relationships.

- How parents will keep records of their child's learning and progress in the off-site element of the agreement, e.g. by keeping a journal including children's writing, parental observations, reports and annotated photographs.

- What arrangements will be made for pupil assessment (see below)

- Which provisions will be made for any perceived special needs?

- What flexibility there will be regarding special events which fall outside the normal attendance pattern.

- How the register will be marked (see section Marking the Attendance Register).

- The length of time the agreement is to run before being reviewed.

- Under what circumstances and with what notice either party can withdraw from the arrangement.

National Curriculum and Assessments/SAT's.

The National Curriculum applies to the school-based

part but not necessarily the non-school based part. The national curriculum does not apply to the non-school based part of the education of a flexischooled child unless this was part of the agreement between the school and the parent.

SATs are a statutory requirement for schools, so the normal rules apply and the child will be expected to sit them all.

Marking the register

We have included this as sometimes confusion over the mark in the register and therefore the attendance statistics for the school puts head teachers off agreeing to requests for flexischooling.

There are currently two options for the sessions during which the child is not physically at the school but being educated elsewhere:

Where the child is part time educated at school and part time electively home educated (i.e., with neither oversight nor approval from the school) then the registration mark used is "C" - authorised absence – for the non-school sessions. Naturally this affects the attendance figures of the school, which can be problematic, but Ofsted takes the stance that so long as the pupils are educated that is what is important.

Where the arrangements meet the criteria for "Off-site educational activity" (see The Education (Pupil Registration) (England) Regulations 2006 regulation 6(4)) then a "B" code can be used which does not affect attendance figures. In order to meet these criteria, the school must authorise the parent to provide the education, and possibly also approve the education that will be taking place. This authorisation and approval may be granted on a termly or annual basis through a meeting or exchange of reports between the school and the parent.

In summary, if the school have authorised the parents to manage the education taking place in the session or have approved the education planned to take place then "B" can be used, otherwise a "C" must be used.

What parents say

"I felt that I wasn't ready or able to offer my daughter full-time Home Education. So, after researching huge amounts found out about this happy compromise. We have not looked back."

"My son goes to a village school about 16 miles away. The school and the head teacher are very, very supportive and fantastic! Nearly half the school is flexischooled."

"They are competent, independent kids, and for me that is a reward in itself. It allows me to have an interesting job for three days, and for them to do their own thing without me, and then we have a four-day weekend when we share our time together and they can follow their own interests."

"We want our children to play, to experiment, to find their passion, to make friends, to be free, to be wild, and to have time. That is probably the most important thing: To have time. Free time. Time to play."

FAQ.

What role do the LA play?

None. But they advise schools (often incorrectly in the case of flexischooling) on the law.

Can I appeal against the head teacher's decision?

There is no appeal against the decision of the Head teacher not to agree to a flexi-schooling request.

I thought the government had stopped allowing flexi-schooling a few years ago?

There was a month back in 2013 during which the then current Minister attempted to ban flexischooling. This was reversed when it was pointed out that the action was unlawful. Flexischooling is not banned and the rules and regulations which allow it to have not changed for a decade if not longer.

What if my child is under 5?

Formal flexischooling does not apply until children reach compulsory school age (CSA – the term after a child turns 5). Up until this point the term used is 'part-time'. Information regarding part time schooling for children under 5 can be found in a separate leaflet... **Part-Time Schooling in England (Under 5)**[xxiii] and reproduced below,

Centre for Personalised Education, March 2018.

4.2 Part-time schooling for children under 5 – in England

Formal flexischooling does not apply until children reach compulsory school age (CSA – the term after a child turns 5). Up until this point the term used is 'part-time' and the attendance requirements are as follows:

The Law in England

In December 2014 the Schools Admissions code (England) **School Admissions Code (England)**xxiv was updated. Children under compulsory school age can now attend part time if the parents so wish. Children are marked absent using code X which means school attendance records are not affected. Below is an extract from page 24 of the Code.

2.16 *Admission authorities* **must** *provide for the admission of all children in the September following their fourth birthday. The authority* **must** *make it clear in their arrangements that, where they have offered a child a place at a school:*

a) *that child is entitled to a full-time place in the September following their fourth birthday;*

b) *the child's parents can defer the date their child is admitted to the school until later in the school year but not beyond the point at which they reach compulsory school age and not beyond the beginning of the final term of the school year for which it was made; and*

c) *where the parents wish, children may attend part-time until later in the school year but not beyond the point at which they reach compulsory school age.*

(By law, a child reaches compulsory school age on the prescribed day following his/her fifth birthday or on his/her birthday if it falls on a prescribed day. The prescribed days are 31 December, 31 March and 31 August.)

Clarification on the term 'part-time' was requested from the Department of Education and the response from Sarah Hamilton was as follows:

Thank you for your email. It has always been the intention that children who are not yet of compulsory school age should be able to attend school part-time where this is what parents want – since children who are not of compulsory school age obviously cannot be required to attend school. We made the recent amendments to the Code because we realised it wasn't being interpreted in his way. We would, however, expect parents to work with their school to agree a pattern of attendance which the parent feels meet the child's needs whilst enabling the school to provide them with a meaningful experience.

The new School Admissions Code came into force on 19 December, except where a different start date is stated within individual provisions of the Code. However, on this issue, whilst the wording has changed the underlying requirement hasn't. The Code applies to all publicly funded schools – academies, free schools and local authority-maintained schools.

Feel free to share this information with your local council, and they are welcome to contact me if they would find that helpful.

Regards

Sarah Hamilton

School Admissions

FAQ.

Can the school specify which days and times a child will attend part-time?

Schools may tell parents what part time arrangements they would like the child to attend but, on the basis, there is no legal requirement for the child to be in school, this cannot be enforced. It is however, worthwhile trying to work with the school to come up with an arrangement which suits both parents and school as there are many years ahead and a good relationship is beneficial to all parties.

Will my child suffer socially because they aren't full-time like the other children?

This will depend on the child and the classmates. It is often raised as a concern by teachers but is generally a much smaller issue than they may believe. At nursery and playgroup most children attend part time, and this is considered normal. The children have got used to friends being there some days and not others. Lunchtime clubs mean that children miss various playtimes and then of course sickness means that children can be off at various times. Friends being absent sometimes is a normal part of school. If it is a concern to you then attending half days and staying for lunch means children are at school for the main play times. Arranging play dates after school can help build stronger friendships as well.

Will my child suffer academically because they aren't attending full-time?

This is possible if a child misses significant parts of the school week. It can easily be resolved however, by talking to the school and understanding what topics are being covered, when and how. This way parents can work out if there are parts of the week where it would be beneficial for their child to attend. Many schools cover academic subjects in the mornings and would, therefore, prefer children to attend then. There may also be regular times in the week when new concepts and topics are introduced, and it could be useful for a child to be there at those times. Some compromise may be the answer so that both sides feel the part time arrangement can work well.

Work missed at school can be covered more quickly at home if parents feel it would be helpful to do so.

4.3 Advantages of Flexischooling

These points are illustrative and not an exhaustive listing.

Children

- Many parents feel schooling starts too early when their children are neither developmentally, emotionally nor intellectually ready.

- Parents of children with autistic spectrum conditions can find flexischooling meets their children's needs better than either full-time school attendance or full-time home education. School experience is balanced with time at home, where school learning is supported while the child's need for a less stimulating environment is also met. The autistic child can also more readily focus on their own special interests, take the processing time they need, consolidate family relationships and have fun.

- In similar way children with a range of conditions like Attention Deficit Hyperactivity Syndrome (ADHD), social communication issues or communication and language processing challenges can be supported. For example, children with sensory overload and significantly slower processing times need that same break to recover, consolidate and move forward. Full-time school can be overwhelming for them.

- Gifted and talented children are often under challenged in schools and as a result may become bored, disruptive or withdrawn. Flexischooling offers the opportunity for them to study at an appropriate level at home while benefiting from the school environment.

- Full-time school is inappropriate for children with some medical conditions. They may tire easily, need medication or their condition may be just too problematic to manage while attending school full-time. Attending school for a manageable amount of time each week allows these children to maintain their friendships and prevents isolation.

- Some children just don't thrive in school. This can have a negative impact on all of their life experiences and relationships. The flexischooling balance is often shown to have a positive impact.

- School phobic children have crippling anxieties which make full-time school impossible for them. Flexischooling has offered many of these children a way back into education.

- Bullied children can often fail to thrive or become school phobic and are often served well by flexischooling arrangements.

- Children from bi-lingual families have found time to value and develop their mother tongue and culture. This has had positive effects on their all-round educational performance and ability to thrive within two or more cultural and language communities.

- Children can access examinations made available in schools. Access to exams is often complex and costly to the elective home educator. In addition, barriers are often created by schools who do not want to accommodate external candidates.

- Tailoring the education to the individual needs of the child by meeting their abilities and aspirations can lead to faster and more sustainable development in such areas as independence, self-reliance, responsibility and self-direction.

Families

- Families, of course, reap the benefits of happy, thriving children who are eager and able to learn. Without the flexischooling option families can be drawn into a cycle of despair, high levels of stress and potential breakdown. Family cohesion and well-being can be significantly enhanced by flexischooling arrangements.

- Some parents who wish to home educate are unable to do so because they need to work. Flexischooling allows them to be involved in their children's education.

Schools

Schools often find flexischooling challenging at first. This is because they often know little about it as accurate information is not readily available. Flexischooling is discouraged by the Department for Education. Furthermore, it is discouraged by Local Authorities who wrongly believe it to be a safeguarding issue. To our knowledge, flexischooling does not feature in any teacher training. If these obstacles are overcome parents may find the head teacher quite positive. There are good reasons for this and the following outlines some of the advantages to schools.

Pragmatism

- Schools are entitled to full funding whatever the balance of school / home-based learning.
- Increased number of children registered at the school thereby ensuring sustainability in very small schools. Hollinsclough is a good example of this.
- A proportion of flexischoolers will go on to take full-time places.

Philosophy

- Teachers want to make a difference, to change lives and develop communities. Meeting the needs of individual learners, through flexischooling, is a great way to achieve this.

- Flexischooling changes lives and has proven to be effective for a range of children and young people.
- Flexischooling parents are usually passionate and highly committed, willing to work in partnership with, and support, teachers and schools.

Pedagogy

- Experience shows that flexischoolers can bring new dimensions and qualities to the classroom. The arrival of flexischoolers, their needs and timetabling has prompted curriculum and learning developments very often advancing benefits for full-timers as well.
- Flexischoolers often have greater independence and self-management, high levels of thinking, communication and questioning skills, creativity and persistence.
- Those settings with larger numbers of flexischoolers have explored high level pedagogical approaches with project based, enquiry-led, research approaches, online e-learning, blended support and so on.

Progress and achievement

- Flexischooling is beneficial for parents, learner and school. Flexischoolers will usually go beyond schooling time frames flexibly utilising evenings, weekends and year-round experiences.
- Normal spectrum and gifted learners can devote sufficient time to their passions and dispositions. Evidence demonstrates that autistic spectrum learners can benefit with the flexischooling balance.
- Other developmental, maturation, physical, learning and emotional needs appear better

accommodated by flexischooling.

- Struggling children can have beneficial one to one time at home. Schools often find that flexischoolers lead to overall gains in their performance and value-added data.

4.4 Challenges of Flexischooling

When seeking a flexischooling agreement families may encounter a number of challenges including:

Information

The likelihood of head teachers being fully informed about flexischooling is quite rare. Most have no knowledge or experience of flexischooling. The first hurdle is providing and pointing them towards information. Without it head teachers will understandably go straight to local authorities where the response may be luke-warm, misinformed or worse.

The Centre for Personalised Education flexischooling website section[xxv] and this handbook should now fill this vacuum for all parties and give everyone the information with which to make their case. It's worth stressing once more that the decision is a local school decision at the ultimate discretion of the head teacher.

Finding a School

It would be impossible to provide a list of every school that will accept flexischoolers. The situation remains that the majority of schools have never been approached and most still do not know of the concept and possibility. Matters are further complicated by some schools and some flexischooling families wishing to remain 'under the radar'. Added to this, contexts will change over time and settings may become more or less sympathetic to flexischooling according to issues like capacity, staffing and so on.

The Centre for Personalised Education is working with others to make locating sympathetic schools easier. It has devised a simple Flexi Mark scheme which we hope will eventually help families and schools locate each other. (Information can be found in **CPE Journal 17 Flexischooling Guidance**)[xxvi]. **With the Flexi Mark schools/settings can advertise the fact that they work flexibly with learners and families in flexischooling partnerships or are open to developing these.** Hollinsclough CE Primary Flexischool is additionally establishing a **Flexischooling Federation**[xxvii] which will identify and work with a network of schools. Eventually we hope we can establish a national network of visible flexischools.

Currently most families will approach a number of schools before they find a receptive welcome. In some areas, this can be a difficult and disheartening process.

Distance

Finding flexischool places in a local school would be ideal, but this is often impossible. However, families seeking the best for their children through flexischooling have shown enormous commitment many have made sacrifices in order to take their children to suitable schools outside their local area. Many home educators are already accustomed to making such sacrifices and employing creative use of their time and resources in order to provide their children with a suitable education. Over time as flexischooling becomes more widely known as a credible option it is hoped that distance will cease to be such an issue.

Teachers

However welcoming and positive a head teacher may be, they are not usually the teacher who will be working with the flexischooler in the classroom. Therefore, it is important that teachers and support staff are also well informed and positive. The head needs to convince the appropriate teachers and support staff. Without their willingness to embrace flexischooling things are unlikely to go well. Teachers are under immense pressure as it is and flexischoolers may just seem like another burden. The head will play their part, but parents/carers who work with the teachers sensitively, liaise with the school and support the arrangement will get the best outcomes. When families are requesting flexibility in their child's education it is only reasonable that they are flexible with teachers and other school staff. The irony is that while many teachers will be sympathetic to parents' requests for flexibility the realities of the current climate and infrastructure make things difficult for them. Parents would be advised to take time to develop positive reciprocal relationships with schools. Many teachers, once they have settled into the routines of flexischooling, report that they find it empowering.

Review

It would be quite understandable for schools new to flexischooling to agree quite modest flexischooling arrangements initially as all parties work their way into the idea.

Alongside day to day informal communication, planning and incorporating regular reviews into the flexischooling arrangement (e.g. every half-term or term) has proven to be mutually beneficial. This allows praise to be given, problems to be aired, solutions to be negotiated and adjustments to be made ensuring that flexischooling continues to work in the child's best interest.

Secondary School

At this moment in time we are aware that flexischooling is more prevalent in primary schools. This situation has probably arisen because the recent surge in families requesting flexischooling has been with primary school aged children and the demand has not yet worked through to the secondary phase. There is no fundamental reason why flexischooling at the secondary level should be problematic. Indeed, in many ways it should be far simpler to organise and facilitate. The scope for real innovation and increased flexibility is excellent.

As the current cohort of primary aged, flexischooled primary aged children get older, The Centre for Personalised Education will broaden the focus of our campaign to include more secondary schools. It should be noted that families currently enjoying primary flexischooling would be best advised not wait until the transition. They should liaise with secondary settings in advance, laying the groundwork and ensuring the intended secondary school is accurately informed about how flexischooling works and that there is a growing demand for this kind of provision.

Other Perceived Challenges of Flexischooling

Hollinsclough CE Primary Flexischool Academy in Staffordshire, have had a great number of flexischooled children on roll in their small school. They researched and dispelled some of the perceived challenges of flexischooling. The following is a summary of their experience.

Unfair on other children.

Children who attend school full-time might resent the fact that their peers do not have to attend five days a week, and get to participate in other activities such as museum and zoo outings while they are in the classroom. In practice, we have never seen evidence of this.

Harder for child to acclimatise to full time school.

Children who find it difficult to adjust to school might find it even harder if they are allowed to spend several days a week at home with their parents. In practice, we have only found this to be the case with children who attended infrequently or irregularly.

Can make it difficult for children to forge strong friendships at school

as they may be absent when the friendships are forged. In practice, we have never seen this. Moreover, children are made to feel really welcome because their friends have missed them.

4.5 Models

Flexischooling models.

There are no fixed flexischooling models. Arrangements are designed to best meet the needs of each child and the contexts and resources of schools. The ratio of school based and home-based learning and access to specific areas of curriculum is decided by agreement on a case by case basis.

Currently schools are held to a rigid set of rules, procedures and targets. This means the scope for flexibility may feel somewhat constrained. Families should bear this in mind when approaching schools. That said, the initial flexischooling agreement will of course be regularly reviewed and can be altered and developed as all parties grow in confidence and security to tailor the education in the best interest of the child.

The largest flexischool in England is Hollinsclough Primary. they have established their own model which works in their context. Details of this can be found on their **Hollinsclough Flexischooling Page**[xxviii]

4.6 Contracts

Just like the models above there is no fixed contract format. That said, it makes good sense for families and the school to come to a formal agreement outlining the flexischooling framework and each party's responsibilities. Like everything else this can be the starting point later reviewed and developed and the agreement amended as necessary. A contract ensures clarity and lays out explicitly responsibilities and duties thereby lessening the opportunity for misunderstanding and conflict.

The Flexischooling Contract and Attendance Agreement

When the decision to flexischool is made the parents

and head teacher should meet to discuss how the arrangement will work. Following this discussion, the contract and attendance agreement can be drawn up and signed (see example later in this article)

Such a contract might include sections on:

- What areas of education each party will provide?
- Who will oversee the non-school part of the education?
- What flexibility there will be regarding special events at school which fall outside the normal attendance such as school trips and assemblies?
- What flexibility there will be regarding special events with the parents which fall inside the normal school attendance?
- What arrangements will be made for pupil assessment?
- Any perceived special needs and associated provision.
- Who is responsible for the welfare of the child?
- To what extent the National Curriculum will be followed.
- Pattern and frequency of review.
- Anything else that the parents and school see fit to include.

The attendance agreement states when and how often the child will attend school.

Examples of contract agreements can be found within the **CPE Journal 17 Flexischooling Guidance**[xxix], and the **Hollinsclough CE Primary Academy Flexischooling website section**[xxx]

4.7 How to Approach Schools

What follows is our latest flexischooling information sheet on Negotiating with Schools. It can also be downloaded here: **Parents Negotiating with Schools**[xxxi]

Flexischooling – Information for Parents Negotiating with Schools.

Please read this in conjunction with our other information leaflets.[xxxii]

Part-time schooling pre-compulsory school age.

Flexischooling is not to be confused with part-time schooling prior to compulsory school age. This is a parental right and must be accommodated by schools **(see Admissions Code (Dec 2014)**[xxxiii] Section 2.16) https://www.gov.uk/government/publications/school-admissions-code--2[xxxiv]

Information to read and have to hand.

We suggest you give copies of this information to the head teacher

Is Flexischooling Legal in England (V1 April 17)[xxxv]

Head teacher leaflet (V3 May 17)[xxxvi]

Link to all our flexischooling information in the CPE website section[xxxvii]

Attendance Codes.

This thorny question is often the deal breaker. Despite

no change in the law recent communications with the DfE have muddied the waters and there is a lot of misinformation surrounding the use of codes. In law the choice of code is the head teacher's and he can use any code he likes so long as he can justify it to Ofsted and the governors. We've outlined the legal situation in our other briefing documents and although some local authorities may try to dissuade schools the fact remain this is achievable and many, many schools make rational and perfectly supportable decisions as to which code they will use.

There are currently two options:

1. Where the child is part time educated at school and part time electively home educated (i.e., with neither oversight nor approval from the school) then the registration mark used is "C" – authorised absence – for the non-school sessions. Naturally this affects the attendance figures of the school, which can be problematic, but Ofsted takes the stance that so long as the pupils are educated that is what is important.

2. Where the arrangements meet the criteria for "Off-site educational activity" (see The Education (Pupil Registration) (England) Regulations 2006 regulation 6(4)) then a "B" code can be used which does not affect attendance figures.

Code B: Off-site educational activity

This code should be used when pupils are present at an off-site educational activity that has been approved by the school. Ultimately schools are responsible for the safeguarding and welfare of pupils educated off-site.

Therefore, by using code B, schools are certifying that the education is supervised and measures have been taken to safeguard pupils. This code should not be used for any unsupervised educational activity or where a pupil is at home doing school work. Schools should ensure that they have in place arrangements whereby the provider of the alternative activity notifies the school of any absences by individual pupils. The school should record the pupil's absence using the relevant absence code.

In order to meet these criteria, the school must authorise the parent to provide the education, and possibly also approve the education that will be taking place. This authorisation and approval may be granted on a termly or annual basis through a meeting or exchange of reports between the school and the parent.

In summary, if the school have authorised the parents to manage the education taking place in the session, or have approved the education planned to take place then "B" can be used, otherwise a "C" must be used.

The role of the head teacher.

The head teacher is ultimately the person who will agree to, or deny, your request. Most head teachers will probably be unaware of flexischooling, so providing them with the relevant information is important.

Certain schools may initially be more open to flexischooling. These might be small schools and undersubscribed schools. Where a school is fully or oversubscribed it may well be extremely difficult to accommodate more children even if they are flexischoolers.

It is probable that the head teacher will also want to take the advice of the local authority.

Role of the LA.

Under ideal circumstances local authorities would have authoritative knowledge about flexischooling but sadly, most haven't. They often give inaccurate advice, sometimes because they don't know about flexischooling and sometimes because they disapprove of flexischooling. Ultimately it is not for the local authority to decide, because the decision belongs, in law, to the head teacher.

First communications.

It is important to direct your initial enquiries directly to the head teacher (office staff may not understand your request or fail to pass it on). You can provide him with the briefing information linked above.

It's useful to cover all bases – some people prefer hard copies, others work digitally. Do both. It's important that head teachers have information so that they can prepare for a meeting. Your covering letter should point to further relevant information that is available on the Centre for Personalised Education website

www.personalisededucationnow.org.uk/concept/xxxviii

Covering letters should be short and to the point. A brief explanation of why you are seeking flexischooling is fine but save the rest for the meeting.

Face to Face Meeting.

Personal communication is essential if confidence and trust are to be built. Make an appointment to meet with the head teacher and ensure there is sufficient time to discuss flexischooling. Although you may be knowledgeable, and perhaps passionate, about flexischooling please don't assume the head teacher will be. The idea may be totally new to them and therefore presents a challenge. Bear in mind that even if the head teacher is convinced by your arguments they will also need to speak to and bring on board the appropriate class teacher(s). If all parties are not on board any arrangements can easily break down.

Try to understand the head teacher's concerns. This will enable you to work more effectively with the head to find solutions. This may seem daunting but the information you have already sent them holds the keys to your arguments and most head teachers would be prepared to engage in a dialogue and look into this further. Rehearse the arguments – include practicalities, why you want to flexischool, how it works and how you will be able to show it is working.

Confidence, trust, commitment.

We can't overstate the importance of a strong personal relationship with the school that provides the class teacher and head teacher with an underpinning of trust. In the context of current schooling and the pressures on teachers there will be adjustments to be made. In one sense, a school could just say 'why should we put ourselves out when we already have so much on our plate.' If you appreciate this and show your understanding of the school's position things will go better.

If your children are home educated you may well need to do some groundwork in breaking the usual embedded home educated stereotypes. The likelihood is you are well used to these arguments anyway. This is important learning for school staff and a worthwhile engagement in itself.

Even if you've convinced the head teacher to go ahead with a flexischooling trial it's in your interests to invest time in building the core relationship with your child's class teacher. If the rapport here is good then it is likely that other staff and the head teacher will be receiving good reports and more likely to be happy with flexischooling continuing in future years.

Curriculum and learning.

Currently schools are driven by the need to meet assessment targets and deliver a prescribed curriculum. This means that school timetables are far more rigid than they may have been in the past. Therefore, the school may require your child to attend on certain days or sessions that fit with the timetable. Whilst that may not be your ideal you may need to compromise to get things off the ground.

Common concerns raised by school and others:

- **Lack of progress / falling behind.**

  This rather depends what you are looking for from the school. If it's the basics i.e. maths / literacy where rigid timetabled progressions operate, then you will need to discuss the timetable to ensure attendance at relevant times. You should also discuss how learning will be supported and developed at home. On the other hand, if it's the non-core curriculum and social experiences available in school that motivate you to seek a flexischooling arrangement, there may be greater flexibility and less concern.

- **Socialisation.**

  An often expressed but thoroughly unwarranted concern. There is no evidence that flexischoolers are any less socialised than their full-time peers. Most socialisation in school is established in the playground, in clubs and extra-curricular activities. Play dates after school and at the weekends can also strengthen friendships. If your child is already at the school then friendships will already be established. Indeed, it should be remembered that school is not the only source of friendship and a child attending school full time still has more hours out of school than in school.

- **Opening the floodgates.**

  This is the belief that when one family flexischools then many others will want to try it. In our experience this is not the case. It is rare for existing full-time pupils to switch to flexischooling, but the school may attract additional pupils when parents who have been seeking flexischooling learn that this school allows it. The very rare schools that have a large proportion of flexischoolers are small rural schools who were previously undersubscribed.

Benefits to the school and the child.

Ensure you are able to rehearse the benefits of flexischooling not only for your child and family but for the school. These are outlined in our briefing documents and on the website. The school will get full-time funding, better motivated learners and parents who are both proactive and committed. Be able to share what you think your child will bring to the class and school.

Children starting later to school or coming from home education can often be more self-reliant, independent, good talkers, questioners, critical thinkers, socially adept across the age ranges etc

Flexischooling means the education can be more personalised to the child, enabling them to thrive mentally, socially, physically and intellectually.

You may have a child with special needs. Schools have the same responsibilities as they have for any registered pupil with special needs. Evidence is growing that for some children with autism, and some other special needs, flexischooling is the best option.

Tour of the School.

If your child is not currently attending the school, it is advised that you get to know the school. Either as part of your initial meeting or soon after it would make sense to arrange a tour of the school with your child. It's important for you to get a feel of the school (rather than just the rhetoric of prospectus and conversation). It is also essential your child can see it for themselves and be included in any decision that may be made.

Contracts.

Clarity is essential and a contract or agreement is a good way of defining this. A contract or agreement may cover

- Roles and responsibilities of both school and parents
- Curriculum (including how much National Curriculum is studied)
- oversight of home-based learning,

- arrangements for assessment,

- special needs,

- welfare and safeguarding,

- flexibilities regarding special events

- review (regular, recurring)

- Termination arrangements

- Arrangements for SATs

- Anything else that either party feels is important

There is **contract guidance** [xxxix] and a number of sample contract templates within our documentation that could be used or construct your own.

Expectations.

You should retain realistic expectations and not assume that you can dominate communication with the class teacher and head teacher. Teachers are relentlessly busy and may be unable to offer you much of their time.

Review and celebration.

This might occur informally in some circumstances on a daily basis; however, formal review opportunities are essential. This may need to be half-termly at least at in the early days, but certainly termly. This enables both parties to give honest appraisal of how things are going and suggest adaptations and a plan to move forward. Reviews also give opportunities to celebrate progress and affirm the arrangement. In some circumstances and with mutual agreement, a home-school notebook or email exchange may be a good way of sharing information. However, be aware that class teachers may not have time to complete these regularly.

Finally.

Flexischooling can be win: win for all parties and has the potential in less constrained times to be transformational in the way schools work.

Centre for Personalised Education, April 2018.

4.8 Testimonies

Arguments aside the reality is we are talking about the lives of children, young people and their families. They deserve the best they can get. We all know some children are not suited to schools and that some schools are not suited to children.

These are just a small collection of testimonies that should prompt us all into making flexischooling work and promoting its efficacy for some families and some schools. The following testimonies are drawn from various members of the Facebook network Flexischooling Families UK.

My boys are now 7 and 10 yrs. old and have been flexi-schooled all through their primary school years.

They attend school on Mon - Weds. They're part of a Wood school on Thursdays. On Fridays, we share a day together as a family, participating in wider learning experiences. Both boys are in the highest achieving groups in their classes. Both are very articulate and bright. Both are thriving in their learning, I believe, because of flexi-schooling, not despite it. Both struggle with the school environment. The boys are both 'highly sensitive'

55

and they just about manage the three days in school. The older son finds school especially difficult as he struggles with sensory overload, especially with a high volume of noise and sounds coming from various directions. All this while trying to follow instructions and stay focussed.

He says he is regularly 'appalled' at the behaviour of some of the children in his class. He says he can't imagine anyone actually wanting to go to school. He is verbally bullied on a regular basis and doesn't feel he fits in. He says he has no friends in his class. He says it's all tests now. (Year 5)

The younger son would rather stay at home as he is very shy, but he does have friends at school and enjoys the sports. He gets distracted easily, however, so is often told to hurry up with his work, which upsets him as he so wants to please.

The school system is not ideal for these children. But both my husband and I work part-time, and it is difficult to see how we could fully home-educate. Flexi-schooling allows for breathing space. It provides the opportunity for a much wider learning to take place, in their much -valued Wood school community, as well as with the family out and about on Fridays, when National Trust properties, museums, art galleries etc. are not busy. We are so very grateful that it is an option. I have no idea what we'll do if it should cease to be so.

My daughter is currently flexi schooling two days a week. We home educated exclusively until 4 months ago, when we decided to try flexi schooling. It works really well for us and she enjoys it and seems to be absorbing information and making friends, losing this would be a huge loss for her and would be very disappointing as it works well but we would never do full-time school as it would be too much for her to cope with in so many ways. I am a Qualified Teacher (Primary and Special Needs) from an EU country with QTS in England, working currently as a one-to-one Teaching Assistant for a child with SEN in mainstream education and as self-employed Music Teacher. I have two boys, 4 and 2 years old, both born in the UK and fluent in English. I have always wanted to home educate my children but as I found myself a single parent when my youngest was still a baby, full-time HE simply isn't an option anymore. Apart from other reasons to choose for home education, I have serious reservations about children learning to read and write when they're only 4 (where I come from, children are 6 when they start Primary School). Now that my eldest is due to start school in September the issue has become rather urgent. When I found out about flexi-schooling I could see how this would work so well for my family. N would be able to access education in English and improve his command of the language whilst at home he could continue to learn my mother tongue which enables him to communicate with his grandparents, uncles, aunts and cousins. Apart from the advantages that come with learning multiple languages at a young age, I feel delaying the education of literacy skills until the child is slightly older has proven to be hugely beneficial to reading and writing skills in the long run. Moreover, my mother tongue is almost entirely phonetic so learning to read that language first will help my son master English Literacy quicker.

Flexischooling is important for my family on an emotional level too. I became a single mum when my (now ex-) husband was abusive towards me which has had an impact on the children's emotional wellbeing. My youngest witnessed a fair amount of verbal abuse and threatening behaviour towards me when he was a baby and can be extremely anxious as a result. My eldest misses his daddy very much and struggles to come to terms with only seeing him twice a month. Neither of them attends nursery full-time and wouldn't be able to. They need the security and stability of home to nurture their emotional needs. Considering what our family has been through, the boys are doing incredibly well and are becoming more confident. It is of great importance for my family that I can continue to provide my children the reassurance of home through flexi-schooling. A final thought concerns the potential choice to home educate the children full-time after all. This would effectively mean becoming unemployed and depending on state benefits. Surely this would cost society a lot more than providing a school with full-time funding for a child who attends part-time?

My son, who is 6 in May, has been attending school for 2 days a week since he started reception. Our reasons for flexi-schooling are basically that we believe that it is definitely the best of all worlds. He thoroughly enjoys his two days at school but also loves his 3 days at 'home'. He is able to appreciate the relative importance of timetables and working on tasks with other children whilst at school and then at home he gets a lot of one on one interaction as well as the chance to participate in a wide range of different activities with the home education community. The arrangement we have is fully supported by the school and they say they have no concerns in the way my son is progressing. His reading is at the level of a 7-8-year-old, so he is not being hampered academically by not attending school full-time. Our family has reached a fantastic balance and we hope to be able to continue this long into the future.

My son who is five and currently in year one has flexi-schooled for the last year and a half. It works perfectly for us and I don't see why it should it change; he attends a lovely small village school and if it wasn't for other children flexi-schooling there then the school may well have to face closure due to such small numbers. My son has been classed as higher ability and has been moved up a year for reading and writing, I'm sure this would not have happened had he been attending school full-time, he goes to school twice a week and is educated at home for the other three days, this i feel works in his favour and would do any other child as they are getting one on one tuition without distraction. I have signed up for flexi-schooling with the school he attends and therefore expect him to continue this agreement until he reaches the age of eleven.

The government should be doing more to support parents' decisions to home educate/flexi-school rather than making it more difficult for us. At the age of two our son was diagnosed with severe autism. In the early years, we tried to follow the normal steps of nursery and playschool, however, we found that without considerable one-to-one adult attention he would wonder and engage in isolating and repetitive behaviours and become ever more distant and anxious. We reduced his time in the playgroup and started an intensive home programme encouraging speech and eye contact and teaching him the foundations across many subjects. When he reached school age he started at a local special school. To help him settle in he started on a part time basis and then after six months he started going full-time. During his time at this school we found that very early on he started to become more aggressive, more insular and rapidly regressed in his academic abilities and speech. We persevered and tried to work with the school to improve things but in the end, we lost all confidence in the school and felt that if he remained there his development would be seriously impeded affecting his entire future, so we felt we had little choice but to remove him and elect to home educate. We have home schooled now for two years and in that time our son has made incredible progress. However, it was never our intention to home school forever and we are very aware that there are certain things that we cannot provide so easily such as group work and social skills. We are very keen for our son to start school and would like him to work up to three days a week. At the same time, we would very much like to supplement this with a continued home programme. We truly feel that such a combination would provide the most effective and beneficial learning programme for our son. At school, he can be around peers, use the specialist facilities, learn to function in the wider social world, try to form some friendships, work alongside others. Alongside this, in a quieter environment at home we can continue to encourage academic development and focus on areas of weakness, things which our son finds difficult enough at home but in the noisy, distracting school environment are virtually impossible. We very much see the two parts complementing each other to meet his needs.

We have heard of people saying that it's the parents' choice to home school but from our own experience we feel this is not always the case and sometimes parents are faced with an educational system that is not structured to meet their child's full needs. To home educate full-time is a physical and financial struggle and yet at the same time the future is very bleak if we are forced to send our son to school full-time and not see him reach his full potential. For us, there is a very real risk that as our son gets older and bigger at some point, we will no longer be able to care for him and he may have to go into care. The thought of this breaks our hearts and yet we have been encouraged by the progress he has made in the last two years and our long-term aim is now that he will develop enough so that he is able to live with us and have some level of independence. For us, this discussion is not about funding, nor about legal responsibility, this is about our son's life and whether he is destined for a future in care or whether he will be given the opportunity to reach his full potential. So, we urge those involved in this process to reconsider and find ways to make flexi schooling agreeable to everyone as we feel it is a necessary educational option.

Flexi-schooling is a fantastic system of education for our family that is enabling our son to flourish academically, physically and emotionally:

- He receives one-to-one attention that is hard to get in a class of 30.

- He gets more time in nature.

- He's not exhausted by the end of the week and has had one cold in 6 months.

- He spends more time with his grandparents.

- He gets to pursue his love of science.

In the last three weeks, he's seen the biggest meteor to land in the UK, dug up a real fossil and controlled a ball with the power of his mind at a Science museum. We know he misses parts of the curriculum but to quote a school Governor "He more than gains from this by what he experiences with his family and that's clear to anyone". Critically, he enjoys school despite the fact he'd rather be at home. It's my belief that 30 hours a week at school would take this positivity away. By keeping his love of learning and experimentation alive, I believe he'll thrive no matter what the world or economy looks like in 15-years' time.

Rowan is a five-year-old with SEN. He is a twin and currently attending a mainstream school, he also has hearing and speech issues and is receiving medical support and we expect him to have some operations this year. Rowan was born prematurely (12 weeks early), him and his twin brother both share a strong emotional bond and enjoy their shared experience of being at a small, village C of E school. They share some friends and are a happy part of a small and supportive community. The school are fantastic, at the moment our son has not got a statement yet and gets 15 hours of support a week which is brilliant but he needs more - flexi schooling would work so well for our son because he stays at the school as his twin but gets the support he so badly needs, he cannot read or write at all and speech is not clear. He could not get any more help from the school; they are doing what they can and we want to help too. We have another meeting with the school next week and hope to start FS soon after but are keeping our fingers crossed regarding recent changes.

The government do not seem to realise that if children like ours are helped by parents now it will cost less for them in the future- even if you take the emotion out of it, it is still a logical solution. There seems to be a lack of trust from the Minister Elizabeth Truss regarding the parents who wish to flexischool when surely it must be only those that are willing to commit who would get involved in teaching their child- I will earn less if we do this but our son needs this. I find it hard to believe that our government would not be fully supportive of parents looking to be so involved in their children's education, especially at a time where we can see how important active parenting is in order to keep children engaged. The question I would want to ask this Minister is what does she want to do with these children who have no statement but are in mainstream schools? If their parents are willing to take the reduction in salary and help what right does she have to tell us we cannot? It's so frustrating because we were so excited to find a solution and now I am not sure what we will do if they decide to not see sense and make this illogical decision, all because of coding it seems, or money, but certainly it is clear that they are not thinking about what is best for a child like ours. I have already organised my work schedule to be free to be with Rowan, and will already see a 20% reduction in my salary. This is not a problem if I am using that day to help our son. The additional benefit for others in the class is that the Teaching Assistants will have time to help other children on the day that Rowan is being taught and supported by me. As he has hearing issues, a silent environment will benefit him greatly but without a statement we obviously cannot have any more provision that we already have.

This is a great example of a positive partnership between school and parents. Of all the issues that need sorting out with our education system, outlawing parents from helping with their child and taking a pay cut in the process should not be one of them. For me, this is a fundamental need that my son has, and without it he is going to fall further and further behind and need more and more resources from an already stretched system.

I am one of a growing number of parents who have chosen to flexi-school because we believe that this is the best way to educate our families. Allow me to explain our situation. When we moved to our current city last April, we applied for a place for our 7-year-old at three local schools. We were sent a letter saying there were no places in these schools. When I phoned and asked where there were places, I was told they couldn't tell me. (It was not until we appealed for a place that we, many weeks later and long after he should have been in school, eventually received a letter informing us of where there were spaces). So, we had no option but to home school. However, during the half term that we home educated our son we noticed and valued a number of aspects of this style of learning. We were able to focus on topics and subjects for longer and explore things in more detail. For example, we chose countries and studied the geography, the culture, the religion, we made the food, the flags and models of the famous buildings. We took creative approaches to developing writing, numeracy, science and general knowledge, attend specific events for home schoolers at the Think-tank Science museum in Birmingham. We could take advantage of outdoor activities, such as forest school and specially organised visits to places like Warwick Castle and the Canalside Community Food project, organised by the Local Home Education Group. We could spend more time on music, art activities and reading together. Our son developed a real thirst for learning, instigating writing and maths activities himself, even at weekends. He became more confident, more relaxed, had more energy and we all enjoyed our time together more. We understand and appreciate the value of curriculum-based education and the huge benefits of the social integration offered by schools, which is why our son now attends school

9 days in every 10. In consultation with the head, in a school not set up for flexi schooling, we agreed that this one day every other week meant that we could ensure he would not miss out on anything at school (indeed we always ensure we catch up on anything he misses), we are able to continue to explore the more focused and at the same time more fluid and creative approach allowed by home education. We believe it to be in our son's best interest. To add to all this, the school our son attends had an Ofsted inspection in October. The report was not good reading and the school was declared to need improvement (something, once attending the school, we were very aware of). While we are seeing evidence of things being put into place to improve the school, we all know it takes time for these changes to take effect. Our children, unfortunately, do not have the time to wait for all of these changes, and flexi schooling is allowing us to ensure that our son is not missing out on his education while his school is brought into line with how the government think it should be.

Through flexischooling I believe children can reap the huge benefits of the education system in this country and also benefit from more hands-on way of learning about their world.

Flexischooling as a tool for supporting education of bilingual children. I do not remember how I found out about flexischooling but when I did I immediately thought it could be a great way of supporting my daughters' mother tongue language without overburdening them with 6 days in formal education (5 days at the Primary School + 1 day at the

Saturday Polish School). I hold an MA in Polish Philology (with teaching) from Adam Mickiewicz University and another MA in Art History from the University College London, the father of the girls is a town planner with an MA in Town Planning and Administration from AMU and MA in Town Planning from the Oxford Brooks University. We both work 4 days a week 9am - 5.15 pm (in our professions). Both my girls are born in the UK. The older one will be 5 in August and started attending school full-time this academic year.

My eldest daughter loves her school, her teacher, she enjoys learning and playing with kids in her class but after she had spent a few months at school we realised that her English takes over her Polish and being apart for most of the week (4 days of my work till 5.15) we missed each other and felt more and more disconnected. Of course, it is important she learns English as she is British and lives in an English-speaking country, but we believe (and it seems the British government shares this belief with us) that she should learn about her heritage and that her bilingualism should be cultivated. Many of our friends in a similar situation send their children to the Saturday schools all over the UK. Being a qualified Polish language teacher, I wanted to teach her Polish myself and avoid sending her to a Polish School but it turned out that time-wise we were very limited - the choice I had was one afternoon with a tired kid or the weekend when everyone wanted to enjoy time with a family and friends. I thought about volunteering at her school facilitating Polish/Art lessons, but it would not be possible to have my younger daughter with me at school. Thus flexi-schooling - having her with me one day a week to teach her Polish reading and writing, let her learn about her heritage and at the same time support her learning through additional activities her school is not able to provide (e.g. going together to the gallery, museum, opera, concert, ice ring, swimming pool, music or theatre classes or various other workshops including these organised for and by local home educators) seemed a perfect idea. I got in touch with the school and we arranged for one day a week away from school for her to take part in an educational pilot project we set up with a group of local parents and with support of the local art gallery. My daughter's teacher asked for documentation and admitted she would love to be able to provide her with all these opportunities we had planned but unfortunately it would not be possible at school. The project has been run for over a month now and we are more than happy flexi-schooling.

Paradoxically I know more now about what she does at school than I knew before as we have more time to talk. She is much more confident now and talks more freely about things. I have time to find out what she does there and support her school learning personalising it and following her interests (e.g. we went to see paintings with Maria and baby Jesus at the National Gallery around Christmas when she prepared the Nativity play at school, this week is the Book Week so we are planning to go to the British Library to see old manuscripts and first printed books, she recently learnt about Carnivals at school and on our off-site workshops she learnt to dance with a dance teacher and make carnival head decorations). During our days away, we also learnt about hieroglyphs and Egypt, met an astronomer from the Open University and learnt about planets with him, learnt about ecology and energy production at the workshop organised by the specialists from the town council, this month we are planning workshops with food specialists, forest school and chemistry workshop, and most importantly we do all of it at the same time developing her Polish speaking, reading and writing skills. Furthermore, during that day when she is not at school, she decides what she wants to do, helps me prepare workshops, meets specialists, other parents, older and younger children, learns from all of them and shares her knowledge with them. She learns that there are different sources of knowledge, modes of learning and different learning environments and most importantly she learns how to deal with them confidently. Being with her I can also support her learning explaining and talking in her mother tongue about things she learns at school and beyond. From what I know about bilingual children's development it is the most beneficial way of supporting her development.

My daughter sees that her parents work part-time so it feels natural to her that she goes to school part-time too and other kids seem to treat it in a similar way. Last time when I asked her teacher for feedback, she had nothing to be concerned about. And I personally feel more involved in her school learning than ever before. I see flexi-schooling as a way of supporting school in their endeavour to provide children with best possible education, with parents offering their time and skills voluntarily to provide their children with opportunities that otherwise would be available only to the kids in paid education.

Our daughter attended school for mornings only for her entire Reception year, as she wasn't five until August. She was very happy and made excellent academic progress. She always had plenty of energy in the evenings for her reading homework and could focus on this well. She started attending full-time in Year 1 and did so until February half term. We became concerned that she had become withdrawn and distant from us, and her behaviour at home deteriorated. She was becoming unkind and aggressive towards her younger brother and sister, crying a lot over little things, and we were finding it hard to communicate with her. We have now been flexi-schooling for the last two weeks, with our daughter attending mornings only again as she did in her Reception year, and we have noticed such a difference. She seems so much happier, she laughs more, smiles more, is more reasonable, much kinder and more caring to her younger siblings, and it is as if a huge weight has been lifted off her shoulders. Our daughter is of a very sensitive nature and worries a lot about things that don't seem to bother most children. She finds it hard to be apart from her family for the long hours of school and becomes very anxious about going to school. We believe her disruptive behaviour at home and her seeming distant from us was the expression of her unhappiness and worries about school. I am a qualified primary school teacher and from my own teaching experience I can see other benefits to flexi-schooling. I feel that full-time school does not allow enough time for child-led learning, nor creative activities, which I believe are very important to a child's development. Flexi-schooling also allows our daughter to spend time on her hobbies and pursuing her own interests. It also means I can take her on outings to museums, castles, country parks and other educational places that provide her with real world experiences and make her learning more meaningful. We have considered full-time home-education; however, we can also see it is beneficial for her to learn to be apart from us and to stand on her own two feet, not to mention the social aspect of spending time with the friends she has at school. By attending school, she also benefits from structured lessons, learning to listen and relate to other adults, being part of her local community, and learning to get on with other children. Flexi-schooling seems to be the perfect educational solution for our daughter as she can benefit from the experiences school provides, without the stress that going full-time seems to put on her. It is very important to us that our daughter is happy and that she receives the best education that we can provide her with, and we believe that flexi-schooling is perfect balance for her needs at this point in time. If we were pushed to choose between full-time school or full-time home education, we would probably choose the home education route, but it would be a real shame if she can't benefit from the benefits of both.

As a trained primary school teacher of 20+ years' experience, it came as a huge shock that my

daughter did not respond well to school. I had never heard of flexi-schooling so for our family it was a voyage into the unknown. Three weeks into the Autumn Term it was clear that, despite an excellent reception teacher and positive and caring school ethos, my daughter was not happy. She had started to 'create' before going to school. First of all, it was in more subtle ways but by October half term her behaviour before and after school until bedtime became almost unmanageable. We knew she was exhausted as she'd willingly gone to bed earlier and earlier each day until she was asleep around 5pm each day. What was as worrying was that she'd lost the 'joie de vivre' that she'd been born with and could not be less interested in almost everything. We'd attended a parent's evening and been told that she was most able and well behaved and that they expected her to do really well. So, we decided to wait and see what happened during the October half term when she was at home all the time. Three days into the week off she had almost returned to her normal self and by the end of the week she was as she had always been bouncy individual with great zest and enthusiasm for life. We literally held our breath on the morning of the return to school and were disappointed but not surprised that the previous pattern of behaviour set in again within days and by the end of the week I had to pries her out of the door in a foul temper. Family dynamics reached an all-time low and we were all extremely stressed and desperately needed to find a solution. We wrote to our head asking if he would be happy to consider having us withdraw her for part of the week and home educate her. I had done copious amounts of research into home education and visited HE groups to talk to people about what life home-educating is like. I was bowled over by the sheer expertise that there was in the HE community and also incredibly heartened that support networks were in abundance and we were most definitely not alone. There followed several meetings with the head teacher, current teachers and eventually her Y1/2 class teacher throughout that term. It was finally decided that yes this was acceptable and that we could commence in the following January 2012. She currently attends school Wednesday, Thursday and Fridays, with one Friday each month off to attend a fantastic HE groups. The school has been incredibly supportive and can see the positive effects this has had on her and the whole family. We have not looked back. Our family life has totally restored its previous happy and settled way. Our daughter is happy to go to school and happy to be at home or out and about with me on her HE days. At parent's evenings, we have been told she's doing well. On the days when she is educated-offsite, my daughter has swimming lessons benefiting from a small number of children in a class, gymnastics after school club when she is fresh as she has not been in school all day, she has pottery lessons one to one with a neighbour in our village who has her own studio, she meets both sets of grandparents for days out, she goes to soft play areas, outdoor play areas, she has been on trips to museums, farms, a Hindu temple, snuggled up in the duvet and read books with me and to her brother for great, happy chunks of time, played properly with her toys, made craft items, written stories, practiced handwriting, danced, played games, romped about in the mud, helped in the garden, used the computer in a multitude of ways, come shopping with us and taken part in every part of our daily lives. She's also really enjoying learning to play the piano and recorder. I have not coerced her in any way to do any of the above it has all come from her general interest in anything and everything. So, in effect, despite my training, I do not find I have to sit her down and teach as she is self-directing. If she asks, I answer to the best of my abilities. If I don't know the answer, we find out together. We have evolved into an autonomously educating family and we all LOVE it!

I have an extremely bright 12-year-old with a very high IQ and exceptional mathematical ability. She got an A star at GCSE maths at age 11. She is currently studying A level maths at home as well as physics and chemistry GCSE. I have been negotiating with some local schools for her to study part time at school so that she can gain socially and take some humanities, arts and foreign language in a school environment. None of our local schools will give her advanced tuition for maths and science, so full-time school is not really an option. Flexischooling seems like an ideal option for a very bright child like mine.

My son has been flexischooled since March 2012. The class he was in had mixed ages - years 3, 4, 5 and 6. The school originally had 2-year groups together but, due to cuts, this had been deemed unworkable, and a class was lost. My son is an intelligent boy but like many, he has a limited attention span and if not kept interested and inspired, he tends to just turn off.

The fact that there were children so much younger in the class caused a lot of problems - we felt that the older children were being 'dumbed down' to cater for the younger children. They were missing out on opportunities that should be accessible to older children, because it was not appropriate for the younger end. This led to my son feeling unchallenged, uninspired and basically very unenthusiastic about school generally. Our first thought was to move him, but in other ways it is a fabulous place to be – beautiful surroundings, lovely staff - plus there was not a viable option within a 10-mile radius. Flexischooling has breathed new life into my son.

He attends school Monday to Wednesday and is home educated on Thursday and Friday. We have a great relationship with the school, which is fully supportive, and my son has absolutely flown over the past year in his levels, in his enthusiasm and in his happiness. When we began flexischooling he was achieving good results at school, slightly above average, but the teacher was aware that he was particularly good at maths, but was perhaps not achieving all he was capable of, they felt he was easily distracted and that he didn't seem to be interested in what he was doing. He was unhappy in, and out, of school. We spent many hours discussing what was best for him and felt we had come up with the perfect solution. The school was happy to support our son and we were happy to keep the school in the loop of what work we were doing. I have just attended a parent's evening and he is already at the levels expected from a child 2 year older - a substantial part of this is down to the work we do at home. We are able to work at his pace, which is too fast for the group he has been with - I am able to stop at the points he needs, or wants, more explanations, and give him that time that was not available to him. Everyone around my son can see the positive impact that flexischooling has had. His reading age went from a year above his actual age to that of someone several years older than him - what inspired him was the fact that we could spend time finding out what he wanted to read - he wasn't limited to what was appropriate for the 7-11's in his class. The favourite discovery that my son has made is that he is really excellent at drawing - he had no idea as it had not been investigated, but we have allocated a set time each week to art and there has been no stopping him! Such a revelation! Looking at a portrait he did a year ago, and one he did last month - the difference is astounding! My son is now a happy and content boy. This is partly because he gets to go through work at home and is then able to carry this same work on at school. If he has a particular area that he wants to go over again, or look at in more detail, he has the chance to do just that with us at home. His mind can move along at the speed that suits, and this has made learning exciting for him! I believe that flexischooling is a viable option for some pupils and parents, those who do want to be within the school system, but who are not getting all they need from that system. If we as parents are willing and able to commit to this important option, then I strongly feel it should be available to us.

I hadn't heard of flexi schooling until last autumn when I stumbled upon an article in the Independent newspaper online. It was a revelation! I have two children with special needs; my eldest has mild autistic spectrum disorder and my youngest attention deficit and hyperactivity as well as social communication issues and language processing problems. To cut a long story short, I feel like I have been on the educational psychologist, occupational therapist, clinical psychologist, consultant paediatrician, child psychiatrist, physiotherapist, speech and language therapist, special needs advisor (and so on!) treadmill for AGES!

My eldest has coped: we have found our path over the years and he is doing well in full-time school, my youngest (aged very nearly nine), not so. He is an excellent school with a great teacher and head teacher and supportive special needs in place. It is not enough. We as parents have tried everything to help him learn, to help him concentrate and attend - from traditional medication to diet intervention to advice from all those specialists listed above(!) - as well as reading probably every published parenting/education book ever written (it feels that way anyway!) – and this is on top of the expertise from my background (I have a degree in education and years of experience of teaching and facilitating learning in children from birth to secondary age) . Nothing had worked for him. Flexi schooling has. And the results were instant. I immediately knew that this was something I wanted to try and the night I read the article I stayed up until the small hours researching. It was the following day I approached the head teacher with my request, for my son to alternate full school days with half school days and have three afternoons a week with me. The head obviously saw that this was a fantastic opportunity for my son to make progress and pushed through discussion with the LEA quickly. We began flexi schooling on a trial basis about a week or so later (we were to review in a month). We have been going ever since, everybody involved (not least my son!) entirely delighted with the arrangement.

My son is academically very behind, and our aim is to develop further his basic in maths and English. We use a well-known tutoring system and at the same time work on these areas (alongside his special needs targets, concentration and listening skills and occupational therapy programme) in a very child centred way. I judge by his mood, his energy level, his interest that day and we take it from there – bringing his focus round to an activity that he can learn from. Last Friday for example, trapdoors were his fascination (he often has autistic-like obsessions) – what did we do in our flexi schooled afternoon? We drew trap doors of various shapes all over the living room floor, we identified and named the polygons, we measured their sides and learnt how to read from the scale on the tape measure and then we used addition to work out the distance we would have to saw to open our trapdoors – he learnt about a perimeter! Would he have learnt as well and as thoroughly in a classroom with individual teacher-led lessons on these aspects of mathematics? No. His interest was there – we snatched the opportunity. Would I like to home educate full-time?

No. I could not. I run a business and need to earn to raise my family. And the benefits my son gets from school, the sense of community, the range and diversity of educational experiences the school provides, the wonderful relationships he has with a range of adults and his peer group, I know I would personally struggle to provide if I was entirely responsible for all this. Would he cope with going back to school full-time? No. He wouldn't. He is calmer, he is progressing, his basic skills are developing at an amazing rate (He can tell the time now! When we started, I thought that was just utterly beyond him!) and this incredibly child-centred individual education from the person that knows him best, his mother, is just the perfect supplement to the education he receives in school.

We came to flexischooling by accident. We had started home-educating whilst living in Yorkshire, as we strongly believed that our son was not emotionally ready for the social experience of school when he reached Reception age. We very much enjoyed this journey together and benefitted from a rich and vibrant local home-education network. However, when we moved to a new region, we initially found it hard to locate local home-educators. We pragmatically decided to ask the local school for flexi arrangements, so our son could meet children his own age locally and get to know the local community. The school had never heard of flexi-schooling, but were very open-minded, with a refreshing attitude that it was our responsibility as parents to decide the most appropriate educational route for our child. We have now been flexischooling for 2 years, during which time my son's education has flourished and he has enjoyed being an active part of two communities – his school-based community and his home-educational one, which we eventually located. Rather than being an outsider, he has learnt how to move between & embrace both of these groups, taking different experiences from both and bringing his diverse educational experiences to enrich each group. Our experiment with flexi-schooling has been so successful, and has impressed the school so much, that last year the school approached me to be a school governor. So, I know find myself in the slightly strange position of being a partially home-educating governor of a mid-sized rural primary school, with growing pupil numbers. With suspicions now being raised that my son might be dyslexic, we are about to embark on a new phase in our flexi-schooling journey. He has started to find his school education days difficult and emotionally challenging, and we hope that screening him for this condition might help us all to improve his educational experiences. We find him to be a very bright and emotionally literate child, who is comfortable in a wide variety of social situations with people of a wide variety of ages. He is stimulated by learning and takes responsibility for developing his own interests – which are not dissimilar to those of other 6-year-old boys – space, dinosaurs, geography & the environment, reading, cycling, climbing and tennis. Flexi-schooling has really been 'the best of both worlds' for my son, a view firmly endorsed by his initially sceptical paediatrician grandmother.

Thank you for all that you have done for our child and consequently for our family - We have taken so many positives from it. We think your school is a very special place to learn and play. I gather from the general hit and miss success of people being accepted in schools to do this (sic flexischooling), that we are lucky. My daughter is 5 and after 2 weeks decided she'd had enough full-time school with huge effect on the family peace. We approached our local primary (about flexischooling) and the head and staff have after several meetings come to accept this as something, they are willing and able to support. Phew! I felt that I wasn't ready or able to offer my daughter full-time HE so after researching huge amounts found out about this happy compromise. We have not looked back. Although this might eventually lead into more home-education and less school, we are very content with the status quo for now. It has worked very well and so far, none of the family have had any problems with negative responses. Let's hope this carries on. Good luck to everyone else pursuing this way of life. PS. My son is 2 and we've decided to do this when he goes to school too!

Our family feels very lucky to have found such brave little school that nurtures the children so well. We originally intended to home educate but then decided to 'flexi-school'... XXX goes to a village school about 16 miles away, the school and the head teacher are very, very supportive and fantastic! Nearly half the school is flexischooled. If we lived nearer to your school, we would attend every day.

I have been flexischooling my 9-year-old since

Easter this year - we do 3 days at school and 2 at home (or not at home usually!) Working very well for us! Although I will continue to home-educate, your approach to supporting my child's needs is beginning to restore my confidence in mainstream education.

I have been home educating my 3 children for the last few years. 6,5 and 3. Yesterday was the older two's first morning at school. We have found an amazing village school that offers flexischooling as standard. They are rare in that they aim to offer a bespoke service as it were to each family. They currently have 5 families doing it. We are going to try a day and a half a week. Despite the tears and protests they loved it. The teacher and I are just trying to work out how best to communicate and work together, since I don't want to feel like I have to do everything in her plan otherwise they may as well be there every day.

4.9 Where can I find more support?

Other information and support can be found here:

- Centre for Personalised Education - website[xl]
- CPE - Flexischooling Families UK -Facebook[xli]
- CPE - Flexischooling Practitioners UK -Facebook[xlii]
- Centre for Personalised Education -Facebook[xliii]
- Home Education and your Local Authority: Help with dealing with officialdom[xliv]
- Centre for Personalised Education -Personalised Education Now (Twitter)[xlv]
- Centre for Personalised Education – Facebook Page[xlvi]

- Hollinsclough CE Primary Academy[xlvii]
- Hollinsclough Flexischool Federation[xlviii]
- Educational Heretics Press - website[xlix]
- Educational Heretics Press -Facebook Page[l]
- CPE - Light on Ed Research Network - Facebook[li]
- CPE - Legal Advice for Educational Startups - Facebook[lii]

Chapter 5. School Information and Guidance

5.1 School Information

What follows is our latest flexischooling information sheet for schools. It can also be downloaded here: Flexischooling (Over 5) Head Teacher's Leaflet.[liii] It should be read in context of the rest of this handbook and the links itemised in 4.8 Flexischooling – Information for Head Teachers

What is flexischooling?

An arrangement where a pupil is registered at school and receives a full-time education but is educated partly in a school setting (primary or secondary) and partly elsewhere (commonly home-based). It can be a permanent, long-term or short-term arrangement. Flexischooling is a local agreement between the school (head teacher) and families. It is a legal option but there is no right to flexischool. This is at the discretion of the school head teacher. See the 'Is Flexischooling Legal?'[liv] leaflet / Chapter 4 for more information.

Why do parents choose flexischooling?

There are many reasons why parents choose flexischooling, such as:

- Parents wish to spend more quality time with their children

- They want an active role in their children's education

- Children can follow their own interests

- Different styles of learning can be respected and accommodated

- Children can benefit from both worlds; being taught at school and being educated at home

- Children who have difficulties attending school full-time, for example because of illness or emotional or behavioural needs, have the opportunity reduce the amount of time spent in school whilst still receiving a full-time education.

At school children can work and socialise with their own peer group, they have access to specialist educators and resources they might not have at home, they can join in with activities such as school trips and plays.

At home children can benefit from individual tuition or small (mixed age) groups, their learning can be self-directed, they can experience a wider range of activities in different environments, e.g. outdoor activities, museums visits

Is flexischooling common?

Flexischooling has been practiced but not widely known about since the 1980s. More recently, a surge in interest and practice has occurred, which means examples of good practice are becoming easier to find and emulate.

At what age can pupils be flexischooled?

The simple answer is at any age, there are examples of successful flexischooling across the full age-range and in a variety of diverse settings

What about under 5's?

Flexischooling is not to be confused with part-time schooling prior to compulsory school age. Children who are not yet Compulsory School Age have a right to part-time schooling if their parents request it (see 2.16 of section 2 of The School Admissions Code December 2014)

Will flexischooling affect my school's funding?

No. Currently all pupils, including flexischooled pupils, registered at a school receive full funding unless they are dual registered.

Does the National Curriculum apply?

Yes, to the school-based part but not necessarily the non-school based part. In law, the national curriculum does not apply to the non-school based part of the education of a flexischooled child unless this was part of the arrangement/agreement between the school and the parent.

5.2 How does flexischooling work in practice?

Models.

There are no fixed flexischooling models. Arrangements

are designed to best meet the needs of each child and the contexts and resources of schools. The ratio of time and access to specific areas of curriculum is decided by agreement. There are schools currently successfully flexischooling one or two pupils and others where the majority of pupils are flexischooled.

SATs

are a statutory requirement for schools so the normal rules apply and the child will be expected to sit them all.

The Flexischooling Agreement.

When a parent is interested in making a request for a flexischooling arrangement, contact must be made directly with the Head teacher of the school so that the proposal may be considered.

Once the decision to flexischool is made parents and head teacher should meet and discuss how the arrangement will work. Following this discussion, a written and signed agreement is formulated between the school and parent in order to make expectations clear for all concerned. The agreement should include:

• The expected pattern of attendance at school.

• What areas of education each party will provide.

• To what extent the National Curriculum will be followed in the non-school based element of flexischooling.

• How school and parents will co-operate to make flexischooling work, e.g. regular planning meetings between parent and school to ensure the child achieves his or her potential and to promote good home-school relationships.

- How parents will keep records of their child's learning and progress in the off-site element of the agreement, e.g. by keeping a journal including children's writing, parental observations, reports and annotated photographs.

- What arrangements will be made for pupil assessment (see below)

- Which provisions will be made for any perceived special needs.

- What flexibility there will be regarding special events which fall outside the normal attendance pattern.

- How the register will be marked (see section Marking the Attendance Register).

- The length of time the agreement is to run before being reviewed.

- Under what circumstances and with what notice either party can withdraw from the arrangement.

Attendance Codes.

As yet, there is no perfect solution for flexischooling in terms of recording attendance. Currently schools can use code B or C. Some local authorities will have their own particular view but ultimately schools must use discretion and satisfy themselves of the best fit for their circumstances taking both the law and attendance guidelines into consideration. This has been confirmed by communications with the DfE. See the 'Is Flexischooling Legal?'[lv] leaflet and Chapter 4 for more information.

Termination.

The arrangement can be ended by either party provided reasonable notice is given. Terminating flexischooling does not automatically mean the child will become a full-time pupil at the school. Families may choose to opt for full-time schooling, move elsewhere and negotiate flexischooling again or adopt full-time home-based education.

What about Special Needs?

Schools have the same responsibilities towards flexischooled children with SEN as they have for any other registered pupil with special needs. Clearly provision will need to reflect the model of flexischooling being operated.

How does Ofsted view flexischooling?

No school is known to have been criticised by Ofsted for allowing flexischooling. The schools we are aware of that have the majority of the children on roll subject to a flexischooling arrangement have been praised for their provision and meeting of the children's individual needs.

Why should schools consider taking flexischoolers?

Schools often find flexischooling challenging at first. This is because of its rarity and the fact that accurate information is not readily available. Flexischooling is not actively encouraged or publicised by the Department for Education. Furthermore, it is discouraged by Local Authorities who wrongly believe it to be a safeguarding issue. To our knowledge, flexischooling does not feature in any teacher training. If these obstacles are overcome parents may find the head teacher quite positive. There are good reasons for this and the following outlines some of the advantages to schools.

Pragmatism

- Schools are entitled to full funding whatever the balance of school / home-based learning.
- Increased number of children registered at the school thereby ensuring sustainability in very small schools. Hollinsclough is a good example of this.
- A proportion of flexischoolers will go on to take full-time places.

Philosophy

- Teachers want to make a difference, to change lives and develop communities. Meeting the needs of individual learners, through flexischooling, is a great way to achieve this.
- Flexischooling changes lives and has proven to be effective for a range of children and young people.
- Flexischooling parents are usually passionate and highly committed, willing to work in partnership with, and support, teachers and schools.

Pedagogy

- Experience shows that flexischoolers can bring new dimensions and qualities to the classroom. The arrival of flexischoolers, their needs and timetabling has prompted curriculum and learning developments very often advancing benefits for full-timers as well.
- Flexischoolers often have greater independence

and self-management, high levels of thinking, communication and questioning skills, creativity and persistence.

- Those settings with larger numbers of flexischoolers have explored high level pedagogical approaches with project based, enquiry-led, research approaches, online e-learning, blended support and so on.

Progress and achievement

- Flexischooling is beneficial for parents, learner and school. Flexischoolers will usually go beyond schooling time frames flexibly utilising evenings, weekends and year-round experiences.
- Normal spectrum and gifted learners can devote sufficient time to their passions and dispositions. Evidence demonstrates that autistic spectrum learners can benefit with the flexischooling balance.
- Other developmental, maturation, physical, learning and emotional needs appear better accommodated by flexischooling.
- Struggling children can have beneficial one to one time at home. Schools often find that flexischoolers lead to overall gains in their performance and value-added data.

Perspectives on flexischooling

Pupil.

'Our teachers are creative, and they always make lessons fun!'

'Flexischooling means I can see more of my mum and we can do loads of really interesting things like go to museums!'

'My teacher really understands us all.'

Parents.

The school offers... 'Flexibility, and appreciation for family life and a respect for learning outside school.'

'You have given him time, space and support to reach his potential and you have accepted him for who he is...'

'None of our local schools will give her advanced tuition for maths and science, so full-time school is not a choice. Flexischooling seems like an option for the very bright child like mine.'

'... she is self-directing... We have evolved into autonomously educating family and we all LOVE it!'

School.

'... from my own teaching experience, I can see other benefits of flexischooling. I feel full-time school does not allow enough time for child-led learning, nor creative activities, which I believe are very important to a child's development'

'... we work closely with parents and view our children's education as a partnership. This is the basis for flexischooling.'

Ofsted

'the school is a leading exponent of the concept of flexischooling.'

'... Good teaching enables pupils from a wide range of backgrounds and abilities to learn successfully.'

'The school enjoys a high reputation among parents who are consulted regularly.'

'Pupils make good progress because of the effective combination of formal, informal and one-to-one teaching,'

'The flexi-school timetable, used to allow individual pupils to be partly home-educated, works very well.'

Centre for Personalised Education, May 2018.

Chapter 6 Additional Notes for Schools

6.1 Flexischooling Models

The school with the most flexischooled pupils in England and Wales is Hollinsclough CE Primary. They have established their own model which works in their context. Details of this can be found on their **Hollinsclough Flexischooling Page.**[lvi] This is only one example and models can vary and be truly personalised for each specific pupil and setting. Different schools may employ different models influenced by such factors as; the number of flexischoolers, the needs of particular learners, curricular provision, online and offsite provisions, help, guidance and so on.

6.2 Funding

Flexischooled pupils have full funding as they are registered as full-time with the school. Their age-weighted pupil formula funding is identical to their full-time attending peers in the setting.

6.3 Registration: The Legal Basis

The responsibility for the education of a compulsory school age child, whether at school, home or wherever is with the parent (The Education Act 1996 s.7).

In addition, the law maintains that pupils should be educated in accordance with the wishes of their parents where possible (The Education Act 1996 s.9). It therefore follows that when a parent requests flexischooling for their child, the request should be approved unless there is good reason not to.

During the non-school based periods of education an appropriate mark must be put in the register. The two options are described in Chapter 4 and the **'Is Flexischooling Legal?'**[lvii] leaflet

6.4 Issues

Unfortunately, flexischooling is not yet defined in law and references to it in DfE guidance and guidelines are scarce and sometimes contradictory. Some local authorities have no policy on flexischooling, and others have attempted to write their own. With so few resources available for them to refer to, it should come as no surprise that the quality of these policies varies widely.

Flexischooling is described in section 5.6 of the Elective Home Education Guidelines 2007 as:

'an arrangement between the parent and the school where the child is registered at the school and attends the school only part time; the rest of the time the child is home educated (on authorised absence from school). This can be a long-term arrangement or a short-term measure for a particular reason. 'Flexischooling'" is a legal option provided that the head teacher at the school concerned agrees to the arrangement. The child will be required to follow the National Curriculum whilst at school but not whilst he or she is being educated at home. Local authorities should make sure that head teachers are made familiar with flexischooling and how it may work in practice.'

A similar definition is given in the School Attendance Guidance (School Attendance Guidance for maintained schools, academies, independent schools and local authorities November 2016)[lviii] which also sets out the marks that should be placed in the register for flexischooled pupils. There are 2 marks available for schools to use: 'B' or 'C' as described.

These issues could be overcome if a new flexischooling registration mark was introduced. The criteria governing the use of this new mark would effectively form a new national flexischooling policy, thus ending the current confusion felt by many head teachers. It would eliminate the need for schools to explain the impact on attendance statistics caused by using 'C'. The contradictions in the current guidance regarding 'B' could be eliminated by removing the requirement for offsite education to take place during school hours bringing it line with reality and home education law. A new mark would also enable the DfE, and others, to collate statistics on flexischooling.

In a flexible society which produces flexible adults, flexischooling should be one of a range of educational models available to all children. The current lack of clear comprehensive flexischooling policy and uncertainty over registration marks, along with head teachers' fears of damaging the school's statistics and Ofsted results, has led to many schools being either unaware of flexischooling or afraid to try it. As a result, many children are being denied the opportunity to experience such a personalised education.

6.5 Special Needs. Gifted and Talented

Special Needs.

Schools have the same responsibilities as they have for any registered pupil with special needs. Clearly, provision will need to reflect the model of flexischooling being operated. Evidence is strongly pointing that autistic spectrum learners can benefit with the flexischooling balance. Other developmental, maturation, physical, learning and emotional needs appear better accommodated by flexischooling. Struggling children can have beneficial one to one time at home. Schools often find that flexischoolers lead to overall gains in their performance and value-added data.

Gifted and Talented (G & T) learners

G & T learners are often given a raw deal with full-time schooling. Their needs are insufficiently accommodated, and they fail to thrive. Flexischooling enables the G & T sufficient time to develop their interests, passions and dispositions in depth and to go far beyond the limited parameters proscribed in the standardised, age-staged school curriculum.

6.6 Advantages, Challenges and Testimonies

As already described in Chapter 4 the advantages of taking flexischoolers are actually quite significant. Aside of the initial learning curve and the generally unhelpful situation regarding knowledge and guidance about flexischooling (which this handbook seeks to address) schools have found the challenges minimal and no more than for any pupil or family. The testimonies from parents in Chapter 4 powerfully describe the impact on learners which any teachers would be proud of. Other narratives about the flexischooling experience can be drawn from schools like Hollinsclough and others in the **Flexischooling Federation**[lix] and discussed in the Centre for Personalised Education Forum for **Flexischooling Practitioners UK -Facebook.**[lx]

6.7 Ofsted

It's worth reiterating to the best of our knowledge no school has been criticised for allowing flexischooling. The schools we are aware of with flexischooling arrangement have been praised for their provision and meeting of the children's individual needs. Indeed, direct communications with Ofsted regarding flexischooling indicate they have no problem with the concept and practice.

6.8 National Network of Flexischools, Flexischooling Federation

The Centre for Personalised Education is working with others to make locating schools open to flexischooling easier. It has devised a simple Flexi-Mark scheme which we hope will eventually help families and schools locate each other. (Information can be found in **CPE Journal 17 Flexischooling Guidance).**[lxi] With the Flexi-Mark schools/settings can advertise the fact that they work flexibly with learners and families in flexischooling partnerships or, that they are open to developing these.

Hollinsclough CE Primary Flexischool has also established a **Flexischooling Federation**[lxii] which will identify and work with a network of schools. Eventually, we hope there will be a national network of visible flexischools.

Chapter 7. Flexi-learners

From the outset its worth emphasising that flexi-learners are no more a homogeneous grouping than the general school population. They come from every social background. Their needs - intellectual, physical, social and emotional - are representative again of the range. Some of the specific groups of children who may particularly benefit have already been described in Chapter 4.

What does make them unique is that they and their parents seek flexible arrangements on which their whole development can thrive and prosper. They are more likely to be responsive and reactive and move to adapt contexts when the need arises. Adapting the education to the individual needs of the child by meeting their abilities and aspirations can lead to faster and more sustainable development in such areas as independence, self-reliance, responsibility and self-direction.

For some, flexischooling is a temporary course of action to support children whose medical, social or emotional needs require a staged re integration into full-time schooling aligning with the child's and parent's wishes. There are many examples of children who have had poor schooling experiences, been bullied or developed school phobias that tried flexischooling elsewhere, have been happy and moved to full-time once more.

There is a whole raft of families who find the UK's emphasis on early formal learning contrary to their beliefs or perhaps prior cultural experiences in other countries. They do not feel their children are developmentally ready for the formality of early schooling and prefer to wait up to 5-7 years before they enter full-time.

In other cases, families have children whose passions and dispositions are being neglected within the mainstream curriculum. Indeed, for some children the lack of stimulation, and challenge, slow progression within learning programmes and inability to follow their own passions creates a whole set of problems. Flexischooling provides a long-term outlet for the learner to develop their talents and interests and mitigates against a fall-off in engagement and behaviours.

A range of specific special needs like Attention Deficit Hyperactivity Syndrome (ADHD), social communication issues or communication and language processing challenges can be supported across flexi settings. Autism (ASD) in particular has proved to be a characteristic where flexischooling is the best of both worlds as a more permanent arrangement. **Dr Clare Lawrence's work**[lxiii] indicates that autistic spectrum learners (and families) may profit from flexischooling arrangements. The intensity of full-time schooling is balanced with time at home to de-stress, process and reprocess learning while the formal structures of an ASD positive school give boundaries and security. The Hollinsclough experience has been that some of the issues that often arise for ASD learners in schools have significantly diminished.

Some children may have medical conditions where temporary flexischooling is a much more effective model. Others may have permanent, chronic or deteriorating conditions that would really benefit from flexischooling.

Families of course reap the benefits of happy thriving children eager and able to learn. Without the flexischooling option some families can be drawn into a cycle of despair, high levels of stress and potential breakdown. Family cohesion and well-being can be significantly enhanced by flexischooling arrangements.

In other circumstances families and children, they have made a conscious philosophical, pedagogical and curricular decision educate 'otherwise' than mainstream schooling. They come from a home-based education background. What has always characterised these communities is flexibility and serendipity. For a range of reasons such as those above some have home-based educated because they felt they had no choice. However, others are fully wedded to the flexibility and opportunities provided by home-based education (for learning and lifestyles) and would not seek to lose that. Sometimes these families and learners do wish to access some mainstream schooling. A range of family circumstances and active decisions taken with the learner might precipitate this choice.

Chapter 8. Local Authorities and Government

8.1 Local Authorities

It's quite easy to feel contradictory emotions towards local authorities (LAs). Many are understaffed, under resourced and often lack appropriate knowledge and training in even the basics of the law. It is therefore entirely understandable that they often get things wrong. At the same time, it is utterly frustrating that they offer guidance and advice which is contrary to the legal position and thwart the aspirations of many families and schools who would like to develop flexischooling arrangements.

The information vacuum and poorly aligned frameworks have led to frequent misinformation and often disinformation and inappropriate interference from LAs. Matters are made worse in times of austerity when local authority officers charged with home education or flexischooling may not be professional educators but less qualified personnel who are more concerned with attendance and data.

Crucially, the current legislative framework for flexischooling (see Chapter 4) does not give local authorities the power to grant or deny permission for flexischooling. The decision to offer flexischooling belongs to the school. That said, schools naturally like to take advice and guidance on issues they are unfamiliar with. Local authorities can therefore play a pivotal role through

their contact with schools.

We have seen many cases where an existing or proposed flexischool arrangement has been hampered by the LA for generally similar reasons. For example, a family may be seeking to flexischool in response to a problem and the LA have a different protocol for dealing with the problem. This may happen when, for legitimate reasons such as social anxiety or bullying, a child is refusing to attend school. The LA then sees the attendance as being the issue and the improving of attendance to be the solution, whereas the family sees the child's suffering as the problem and wishes to alleviate that whilst retaining access to education.

Even in cases where flexischooling is being sought as a so-called positive choice rather than as a solution to a problem, LA staff may see attendance statistics as being more important than educational and social benefits to individual children.

Additionally, because flexischooling arrangements (ongoing or proposed) only tend to come to the attention of the LA after problems have arisen, the LA may have come to see flexischooling as problematic.

Ultimately, flexischooling offers huge benefits for many learners. Local authorities should be equipped with accurate information regarding flexischooling and encouraged to develop clear policies and guidance to support school decisions. A good starting point would be to ensure that on entry to school, and of course at transition stages, families are aware of alternatives to full time school such as home education and flexischooling and that information regarding the alternatives is accurate and comprehensive.

8.2 Government

The Department for Education (DfE) is an extremely busy department and so it is easy to see in the context of other agendas, capacity and so on why flexischooling slips down the agenda. Our own conversations with the DfE confirm this, despite being positively received.

Nonetheless there are some pressing issues:

- Guidance and advice around attendance and registration currently fail to acknowledge flexischooling as a viable option
- The DfE do not promote flexischooling as a proven, effective route for children and families in many circumstances
- Flexischooling is not presented as a model for sustainably supporting small, undersubscribed schools and communities despite the evidence (see Chapter 9).

Chapter 9. History and Potential History

Flexischooling already has a long history and huge further potential to transform schooling for many learners and families.

9.1 Flexischooling, Personalisation and New Learning Systems

Flexischooling has been around in the UK from the late 1970s. But what is it? What does it mean? What could it be? The Centre for Personalised Education has long argued that it has huge potential to our learning system and that it should be recognised as a credible and viable option to families and learners. Flexischooling stands at the boundary between mainstream and alternative or home-based approaches to learning. As such there is the prospect to develop a dialogue between the two and a learning system fit for the 21st Century.

9.2 Origins

As an authentic educational freethinker, our late colleague, mentor and trustee of The Centre for Personalised Education trustee, Prof Roland Meighan was second to none. The idea of flexischooling came to his attention in the 1970s in two ways at once. Dr Meighan was researching home education in UK and found that home educating families were not necessarily opposed to schools. Those who were not wanted a flexible relationship with schools 'getting the best of both worlds'. Some pioneers like Kate Oliver in

105

Warwickshire achieved a flexischooling arrangement with the local school and Local Educational Authority. At the same time Roland Meighan came across experiments in the USA with flexible learning arrangements called Independent Study Programmes or ISPs. It was, in effect, a version of flexischooling. Dr Meighan continued to explore the logistics of flexischooling and additionally held discussions with John Holt in 1984 on the latter's last visit to England before his untimely death from cancer. The culmination of this thinking led to a book in 1988, 'Flexischooling – education for tomorrow starting yesterday', published under the Education Now imprint.

At the same time Philip Toogood, another of The Centre for Personalised Education's late trustee/directors, was headteacher at The Small School, Hartland in Devon. He was invited by the Schumacher Society to co-ordinate a movement to become known as the Human Scale Education Association in 1985, culminating in a three-day international conference in Oxford. This explored the ideas of **minischooling**[lxiv] and flexischooling in a variety of settings including the 'New York City as School' and the need to protect small schools and the right to home education. Philip and his wife Annabel spent two years working at the Small School at Hartland. They were then asked in 1987 by parents to re-open the Dame Catherine's School at Ticknall, Derbyshire, as an independent, parent-cooperative learning centre and all-ages, flexischool. The secondary section of Dame Catherine's split off to become the East Midlands Flexi college in Burton upon Trent; a base for the development of flexischooling (perhaps the UK's earliest example of a full flexischool). This was presented to the Blair government as a model for attachment to each secondary school in Burton but, in spite of initial encouragement to make the application and strong approval in the official published inspection, the request was refused.

9.3 Today

Ever since these early days the Centre for Personalised Education has received continuous enquiries about the availability of flexischooling and how to go about it. The broadsheet newspapers have featured flexischooling usually very positively. Unfortunately, they have not really followed up and developed the narrative on the potential implications of flexischooling. They have also, sadly been prone to stereotype flexischooling families as quirky, wealthy, middle-class, part-time, home-based educators. These myths are quickly extinguished if one follows the flexischooling Facebook groups.

We have been made aware of and supported various flexischooling ventures around the country and fielded many queries from head teachers and governors. In terms of government guidance there is little, and this has hindered the development of ideas. Failure to address real practical issues; legal responsibilities, funding, registration etc. has made things messy for schools, families and local authorities and difficult for those not prepared to go the extra mile.

Matters have been worsened by a lack of understanding of flexischooling. It is often portrayed as a rigid concept rather than a continuum of varying provision. At its simplest flexischooling is a transaction of shared time between home-based learning and school learning.

More radically it can offer challenge across all dimensions of schooling including notions of curriculum, learning and teaching.

Despite these issues, over recent years there does appear to be a growth in flexischooling in all its guises. Mainstream schools like **Hollinsclough CE Primary**[lxv] in the North Staffordshire Moorlands (Head teacher: Janette Mountford-Lees) and **Erpingham CE Primary**[lxvi] in Norfolk have both had extensive media coverage. Clusters of schools in various local authorities are known, as are isolated examples across the country. There are also settings offering different types of flexitime experiences split between mainstream school and some form of alternative learning centre; then again between home-based learning and a learning centre **Self -Managed Learning College**[lxvii] (Prof Ian Cunningham). The permutations are endless.

Are these indications of a shift from the ad hoc to a growing trend? The truth is we do not know. It certainly feels like it. The interest generated by the **CfBT Flexischooling Conference in 2011**[lxviii] was indicative of something stirring. The more we look into the current state of flexischooling the more we find going on.

What is most exciting is the potential we have to harness and network families, learners and flexi-settings. There is an urgent need to develop ideas and practices that can build on the real requirements of learners, on what we know about learning and the development of sustainable families and society. Fleshing out the possibilities offers the chance to develop diversity and choice in the learning landscape and achievement for our young people.

9.4 Meeting Learner Needs

Flexischooling has broad potential for learners and families. Every young person has the right to expect their needs to be accommodated if their learning is to flourish and if they are to make life-long contributions as responsible members of society. A number of learner groups have particular problems in the current systems. They are typically those at either end of the achievement spectrum for whom the age-stage, paced and progressed curriculum and assessment is far too inflexible. They find themselves as 'square pegs in round holes.' Those on the autistic spectrum or those who are exceptionally gifted are particularly ill-served. Flexischooling arrangements can provide a framework for them to thrive, meeting both their specific learning requisites and their social needs. (See Clare Lawrence's article on flexischooling and autism in our **Journal 17**[lxix] and her book **Autism and Flexischooling, A Shared Classroom and Homeschooling Approach**,[lxx] published by Jessica Kingsley.

9.5 The Flexischooling Continuum

We argue that flexischooling (like personalisation) sits along a continuum. At its simplest most basic it is a flexitime arrangement where the school-based and home-based learning are discrete and continue as 'normal'. The mainstream system has traditionally accommodated this to some extent with nursery and early years provision. There are also examples of some secondary phase schools who offer flexitime contracts with various students who earn the right to study away from school for periods.

In the USA flexible week arrangements in Independent Study Programmes (ISPs) use specially trained staff who negotiate timetables with families. So, even in this structured model the concept begins to question some basic assumptions of schooling, for example

- The necessity of a single location
- The role of parents
- The need for teachers to be present whilst children and young people learn
- The relative values of facilitation and formal instruction
- The range of viable resources (i.e. both physical and virtual)
- The necessity of treating everybody the same rather than respecting individual learning styles
- The necessity of having the same curriculum for everybody

At the other (less traditional, more transformational) end of the spectrum flexischooling goes further in confronting notions about schooling and its view of learning. As such, it has very strong links to true personalisation (as opposed to the government's weaker version of personalisation described as 'tailoring'). This type of flexischooling, like true personalisation, recognises the rapidly changing world, the ubiquitous availability and ease of knowledge access, the complexities of life and behaviour. It recognises rigid people do not cope, flexible people have a better chance. Behaviour in the modern world is so complex. Sometimes we need authoritarian behaviour (knowing when to take orders/give them), sometimes times we need self- managing skills of autonomous behaviours and at yet at other times the cooperative skills of democratic behaviour. The world is multidimensional whilst our schools for the most part are unidimensional offering predominantly authoritarian experiences.

Flexibility in all dimensions then, is the key - for example the idea of curriculum. Schooling takes curriculum for granted as the National Curriculum. With its pre-ordained age-stage progressions and assessments. Yet it is, in reality, just one curriculum offer. It is in effect part of what we refer to as a Catalogue Curriculum (a concept described by Roland Meighan in many of his books comprising a wide offer with many options), available from variety of countries and organisations across the globe. Additionally, there is of course a Natural Curriculum which is the learning chosen by self-managed and autonomous learners. It may or may not include elements from the Catalogue. Forward thinking flexischools can begin to explore these dimensions by supporting the learners in their navigation through curricular options and progressions. Rather than the predictable current 4-19 Pathways learners can identify much more flexible learning episodes and journeys at a pace and timescale dictated by their own needs.

In Dr Meighan's conversations with John Holt, John re-iterated his proposal that schools could be invitational rather than based on conscription, somewhat controversially referring to school as a 'day prison'. He said, 'Why not make schools into places where children would be allowed, encouraged, and when asked, helped to make sense of the world around them in ways that interested them?'

9.6 Potential

The flexischooling continuum provides the basis for endless potential and possibilities. It can range from simply and pragmatically meeting needs of individual learners and families currently struggling with the schooling system as it stands, to stimulating transformational dynamics within the system itself. The current schooling landscape purports choice, but the reality is nothing more than superficial. The opportunity to explore new and alternative ways of educating are substantially left to those on the margins, but in reality, this choice is superficial. One has to look at alternative schools and settings that have continue to plough a different furrow but whose very existence is often financially precarious. Flexischooling does permit settings to rethink how they shape their educational offer and work in partnership with parents. They can do this on a sustainable footing and become a catalyst for the wider system.

9.7 School Places

Additional flexi-learners offer undersubscribed schools the opportunity to fill surplus places and to draw in families from a larger catchment area. Families seeking flexischooling are often more than willing to travel extensive distances to come to a flexischooling arrangement with the right school. They prove to be very enthusiastic and supportive parents.

Clearly, flexischoolers present the opportunity help schools remain sustainable, maintain staffing and provision for all the other pupils.

Thinking more creatively, flexischoolers can be a catalyst for a range of innovative and imaginative possibilities for settings to consider:

- Virtual learning hubs which could offer blended learning opportunities / support for all learners.

- Alternative ways of working for some of the time.... e.g. learners negotiating their own personal learning plans and more self -managed learning.

- Development of real personalisation strategies.

- More flexibility with curriculum and less reliance on standardised curricular, age-staged progressions.

- Rethinking and transforming schools… shaking off notions 'one-size fits all' and broadening the educational offer of community-based settings.

9.8 Small Schools

Some schools have reached the situation where the majority of their pupils are flexischooled **(Hollinsclough CE Primary Academy**[lxxi] and **Erpingham CE Primary School**[lxxii]) while most may only have a few flexi - learners. Either way its win: win for learners, families and school. Hollinsclough went from the smallest school in England (3 pupils) to an oversubscribed thriving school (50+). There are plentiful accounts of happy and successful learners and delighted families.

Here is a proven, replicable opportunity to build small schools and maintain the life blood of the local community. Whilst some adjustments will need to be made by all parties, flexischooling is a local agreement between the school and family who will draw up a contract of respective responsibilities and commitments. These are subject to continuous review and development.

The evidence indicates that families are prepared to travel long distances if necessary, to access flexischooling which is a reflection on the rarity of opportunities to flexischool and the dedication of families to the concept. The character of flexischoolers varies enormously. Some children and young people have been to school others have not. Some need more flexible routes to accommodate their special needs or giftedness; others come from home educating families who would like to access some mainstream experience. Some children will also come from migrant families whose educational traditions in their mother country have a later start to full-time education. Other children will be from native UK families who consider school starting age too early or who have philosophical reservations about full-time schooling. There are extensive and growing social media networks with families seeking and sharing flexischooling experiences.

9.9 Home Education Support

In some areas of the USA schools are required to offer local home educators support and resources. Could this happen in England and Wales? On the face of it this appears to be a good idea. A much misunderstood, zero funded community would have the opportunity to share their educational philosophies and needs and mainstream schooling address some their stereotypes and misconceptions. The opportunity for a meeting of minds and mutual benefit could arise.

However, with the history of home education and local authorities and government in England and Wales it would not be popular with all from the home education communities. It would be viewed with suspicion and concerns that schools and authorities would engage in a mission creep designed to bring all home educators under the influence and monitoring of schools.

It would be a sensitive development that required proper consultation and understanding. Technical funding issues would also need to be resolved as currently learner funding is directed solely to those registered at a school and not the home educated.

On balance, currently it is likely that those home educators who entertain flexischooling would probably have little objection and it would be a positive development to the resource they could draw upon. Those home educators who wished to keep totally away from schools and retain their legal right to autonomy would carry on as they always have done. Perhaps a dual model, like that in British Columbia, would be a good idea. There the home educators and flexischoolers can obtain funding in return for closer monitoring or retain their independence and privacy by forgoing the funding.

9.10 Alternative Provision

There have always been children and young people for whom school has not worked either on a temporary or permanent basis. They have had access to alternative provisions varying hugely in their resource, capability and success. At their worst, there have been shocking settings where 'problems' have been hidden and largely forgotten. At their best, there have been settings with some of the most creative and innovative programmes and ideas that have saved and transformed lives.

Flexischooling opportunities blended with self-managed and self-directed learning, individual learning plans, distance learning, work experience programmes could develop to support a range of these children and young people.

9.11 Journeys and Episodes

Professor Meighan took flexibility to completely new horizons when postulating his notions of Learning Journeys and Episodes. The researcher-learner-traveller would become active in co-creating and self-directing their own educational experience and pathways within the wider educational landscape. Effectively choosing to adopt a range of package and bespoke learning pathways as required. He also looked to the evolutionary transformation of schools into all-age Community Learning Centres (CLC) open 24/7 and all the year round. These ideas will not be developed within this handbook but will be covered in other flexischooling publications in due course. Readers can get a flavour for these in the following references.

(Meighan (2004) Humphreys (2014a/b/c/d).

9.13 World Flexischooling

Dr Samantha Eddis - Flexischooling in Arizona, USA (First published in the Personalised Education Now Journal 17. Special. Flexischooling Guidance)[lxxiii]

Flexischooling is just not an issue in many countries around the world. Samantha's four children have experienced flexischooling (dual enrolment) in Arizona over the last seven years. Her experience offers an invaluable perspective. The common-sense attitude of the authorities is to be applauded.

Home-education had never been the plan. After all, I was a qualified teacher, and I have always loved being in the classroom. In fact, we fell into home education in Florida primarily because the local school would not allow my eldest daughter to attend the appropriate grade as she was too young. So our home - education journey began twelve years ago, and even though I was a teacher, I felt completely out of my depth, isolated and lonely, in my new home education life.

I also found it difficult to gel with the home-educating group that I joined. The families were pleasant enough, and my children enjoyed the field trips and social events. However, it irritated me whenever I heard a group of parents extolling the virtues of home education by bashing the teachers in the local schools. The worst comment I heard still makes me cringe, 'Well, home educators are obviously more concerned about their children's education.' Go say that to a family who invests time, money and effort into their child's education, social and sporting activities, and see what reaction you get! That is what I thought, but instead, I simply interjected, 'I'm a teacher.' Funnily enough, the parents shuffled their feet, the conversation shifted, and I wasn't really part of the conversation anymore. Was I considered the 'enemy'? An 'infiltrator'? I wasn't really sure, but I was indignant enough not to care. Fortunately, there were a few families that did not see me as a threat to their home educating lifestyle, and I formed friendships that have lasted to this day. They could see that I was, and always have been, an educator that has seen the benefits of both school and home education and has opted for the best path for my children and my family. I don't judge other families for the way they home-educate, or if they access schools for flexischooling opportunities – I am just following my children's educational needs and desires.

So, our family had five years in Florida, where the home-education laws are not too intrusive, and where we mixed almost exclusively with a small group of like-minded home-educators and the local neighbourhood children. I accessed the local school when my young son was having speech issues (most common in boys, and very easy to overcome when treated early enough). My rationale was that, as an untrained speech therapist, I was in need of some professional help for my son, and my taxes supported the school that my son would have gone to anyway. Not that I foisted such an aggressive perspective on the school. Instead, I asked the local school for help and explained that I really need some professional input – within the week my son and I had seen the speech therapist and we were given some exercises and reassurances that all would be well (and it was).

When we moved to Arizona, seven years ago, I thought more about the common-sense approach of accessing the local school when something was beyond my normal capabilities (speech therapy, specialist reading help, music, art, group PE classes and more). I also looked at the Arizona law, specific to home education. This is what it says, under the Arizona Revised Statutes:

ARS§ 15-802.01 Homeschooled children; eligibility to participate in interscholastic activities

A. Notwithstanding any other law, a child who resides within the attendance area of a public school and who is homeschooled shall be allowed to try out for interscholastic activities on behalf of the public school in the same manner as a pupil who is enrolled in that public school. Registration, age eligibility requirements, fees, insurance, transportation, physical conditions, qualifications, responsibilities, event schedules, standards of behaviour and performance policies for homeschooled students shall be consistent with those policies established for students enrolled in that public school. The individual providing the primary instruction of a child who is homeschooled shall submit written verification that provides:

1. Whether the student is receiving a passing grade in each course or subject being taught.

2. Whether the student is maintaining satisfactory

119

progress towards advancement or promotion.

B. A child who is homeschooled and who was previously enrolled in a public, private or charter school shall be ineligible to participate in interscholastic activities for the remainder of the school year during which the child was enrolled in a school.

C. A school district shall not contract with any private entity that supervises interscholastic activities if the private entity prohibits the participation of homeschooled children in interscholastic activities at public, private or charter schools.

NB 'Public school' in the United States is the state-funded school that is freely available to all children residing in the school district.

Armed with the law in case I needed to refer to it, I went to my local elementary (primary) school and asked if my homeschooled (this is the preferred term in the US) children could take part in any activities at the school. I was amazed by the refreshingly inclusive approach by the school's administrator. She told me that the school district did indeed 'dual enrol' (their term for flexischooling) and then she gave me a list of all the activities that my children could take part in. No pressure was put on me to choose all or any of the subjects on offer, or to bring my child in every day. My children had a card that they gave to the administrator when they went into a class, and then took back when they left the school for the day (school policy dictates that school personnel know who is on campus). When my children expressed a desire to drop one of the classes, we discussed their goals, and then followed the best educational path for each child. As much as I let my children have a certain amount of autonomy with their classes, I was respectful enough to always let the school know if one of my children was going to be absent or drop a class.

Under Arizona law, home-educated children do not have to take any standardised annual testing, and there was never pressure put on me to have my children tested at the local school. Unfortunately for them, as a teacher, I like to have a measurement of my child's academic ability – so I had each of my four children take standardised annual tests, from 3rd grade and above, either at the local school (they were happy to oblige, especially as home- schoolers' scores do not affect the overall scores of the school) or at a homeschool centre in town.

Each of my four children had access to the local school, and to the subjects I felt would be best taught in a group setting: music, art, and PE. There were also opportunities to go on field trips with their assigned class, or attend the sports day and charity events. Just to give you an idea of how each child took what they needed or wanted from the school, I have detailed their flexischooling options below:

First daughter – was only interested in art, so took two terms of art classes in 8th grade. She was not interested in dual enrolling in any other classes, and did not want to pursue options in the high school.

Son – tried music classes but wanted to do his own thing so asked to drop the class (grade 8); took art for a year in Grade 7; took PE for two years (grades 6 and

7). He looked at various sporting options and computer graphics classes at high school, but the timing of the classes did not coincide with his workday at home, so he did not take up dual enrolment options at high school.

Second daughter – went into the local school full time in 1ˢᵗ grade, but came out to home-educate and dual enrol in music, art, and PE in 3ʳᵈ grade. She went back into the local school full time for 4ᵗʰ grade, but then dual enrolled in music, art and PE in 5ᵗʰ grade. She went back into the local school full time for 6ᵗʰ grade and is still in school, full time, in 7ᵗʰ grade. She plans on coming out in 9ᵗʰ grade to dual enrol and take IGCSEs as a private candidate (home educator).

Third daughter – dual enrolled in the local school from 1ˢᵗ grade until 4ᵗʰ grade (music, art, PE) when she went into the local school full time. She is still in school, full time, in 6ᵗʰ grade but also plans to come out and dual enrol as a home educator taking IGCSEs and accessing the local high school from 9ᵗʰ Grade onwards.

I know that I have been so fortunate with our home-educating journey. I have been able to largely accommodate my children's wishes for home education, full-time schooling, or dual enrolment (surprisingly they didn't want to take annual tests!) – thanks, in part, to the common-sense approach of Arizona lawmakers and school district personnel. They have realised that if home- schoolers are committed to providing the best educational program for their children, their school system can offer support and encouragement for an alternative education. I do hope that other home educators who wish to access the local schools or colleges are able to use the experiences of other collaborative projects in order to provide the best education for their children.

Samantha Eddis, PhD, has been teaching for over thirty years, in three countries (Hong Kong, England, and the USA). Passionate about education, and open to the best educational paths for her children, she has also been home educating (including flexischooling) for the last twelve years, in Florida and Arizona. Her focus at the moment is on accessing IGCSEs and A Levels for her children and for other private candidates. Her **website**[lxxiv] gives plenty of free information and suggested resources and her contacts so that other home educators and private candidates can be successful with examinations. She is always open to ideas, advice, or suggestions that will help fellow home educators and private candidates.

Sharon Currie - Our Virtual Flexischooling

(First published in the Personalised Education Now Journal 17. Special. Flexischooling Guidance)[lxxv]

Sharon shares her experience of educating her son Greg. Faced with a range of challenges that make the traditional school environment impossibility, Greg appears to be thriving on virtual flexischooling.

When we took our son out of school six years ago, we had a child who not was not only depressive but also school phobic. Until the present, he hadn't got a good memory of school. His capabilities were such that he was tested for giftedness, but his Asperger's Syndrome worked against him. In the recent years, we realised it was not just Asperger challenges our child had to deal with, but also Sensory Integration Disorder. We also discovered that he suffers from tree and grass pollen allergies being partially responsible for his topsy, turvy sensory integration system. Knowing what we know now, we could see how school was a very scary and confusing place and could not possible work for him. When we removed him from school and started homeschooling, we found all his learning difficulties disappeared. What was left behind was a highly intelligent child with a very distinct learning pattern.

Greg is a kinaesthetic learner. He needs to be moving when he is doing anything. He cannot handle sitting still and doing worksheets but he can solve maths problems super quick when bouncing on a gym ball. He responds best to computer screen learning. In fact, all his learning was done via the computer, bouncing on a gym ball.

When he is learning, there cannot be any other distraction as he struggles with listening if there are other people talking in the same room. Instructions have to be given verbally and then reinforced with text (just like watching television with subtitles on). We suspect Greg has auditory and visual processing issues. Hence, over the years, we have supported Greg's learning through online educational programs and private tutors.

It has always been Greg's ambition to go to college. This year saw him starting first year of high school. It will be impossible for Greg to survive a physical bricks and mortar school - the sensory overload would totally overwhelm his senses. The loud noises, the crowds; scratchy uniforms, smells, lights and the multitude of distractions in classrooms would all work against him.

Flexischooling seems to be the only option to us. We chose virtual schooling and decided on **InterHigh Virtual Highschool** [lxxvi]

So far, Greg is enjoying himself. Lessons are from 9.30 - 11.45, with a 15 minutes break in between, Monday to Friday. Homework is issued daily. Every morning, after breakfast, he logs into his classroom from the comfort of our living room. There is no audible sound from his classmates only his teacher. This clarity allows him to listen and understand everything being taught easily. If he has any problems, he can privately text the teacher his questions. When he gets stressed, he can move about the living room, without having to leave his classroom. It is important for Greg to keep moving, as this will help his brain understand of what is being taught.

Greg is also doing ICT classes with **FunTech,**[lxxvii] a local ICT academy in Maidenhead. This is where he will be sitting his ICT GCSE exam too. At the moment he is attending classes physically but there is arrangement being made for him to do his ICT lesson virtually in January 2013. Once this happens, Greg will be able to do his lessons virtually anywhere - even when we are travelling.

We felt flexischooling is the way forward for our child. It allows him to continue to learn without unnecessary stress. It also allows us the freedom to travel. We feel travelling is an important part of his education. The flexibility also allows Greg plenty of opportunity to pursue his own interests such as music lessons in guitar, drums and piano; swimming; museums visits; meeting friends.

Technology is amazing and has made it possible for my child to learn outside school. When we travel, he logs into his virtual classroom on the internet, on his laptop, via our iPhone hotspot function. Learning has no boundaries now for my kid. School doesn't have to be a bricks and mortar building anymore.

Sharon is a full-time housewife, mum, carer and homeschooler.

'My days revolve around Greg and his needs. I'm an avid reader. My reading interest is very much focused on the subject of Autistic Syndrome. I read about how the right environment, the right attitude and the right diet can help make everything better and easier for an autistic person. It's about how to enhance their unique autistic abilities rather than disable or limit their capabilities. As practicing Buddhist, meditation and pursuing online Buddhism studies are very much part and parcel of my life too. Finally, when I do get some free time, I like to knit, crochet and paint.'

Dr Fatima D'Oyen - Reflections on Flexischooling (First published in the Personalised Education Now Journal 17. Special. Flexischooling Guidance)[lxxviii]

The success of an education should be measured by the people, lives and societal contributions it produces. Fatima is in the rare position of having experienced a flexischooled education as a learner in the USA built her own flexischooling setting with the Manara Academy in Leicester, UK (now ceased as Fatima has returned to the USA). Her insights and reflections are powerful in advocating a less rigid system.

In 1974, when I was fourteen, my world was turned upside down: three of my grandparents, one of whom had raised me from a young age, died within six weeks of each other. I suddenly found myself uprooted from my home in suburban New York, needing to adjust to the slower pace and warmer climate of Albuquerque, New Mexico, in the south-western USA. Besides the personal adjustments required, which were substantial, there was the problem of schooling: New York City had perhaps the best public (state) school system in the States, and New Mexico one of the worst. NYC also streamed children by ability in those days, and I had been in the top class. My father convinced the principal to move me up to a higher year group, but that didn't help. My former classmates had often talked about which universities they hoped to attend and how much money their relatives gave them for achieving as on their reports. In contrast, I was taken aback to find several of the mostly Hispanic 14-15-year-old girls in my new class comparing their engagement rings while the teachers' words went above their heads – or, in one ear and out the other. In the end, my father decided that home-education might be a better option.

However, my father and stepmother were not in the position to provide me with a suitable home-education, so we were all interested to hear of a new kind of school, Freedom High School, where students only went to school for half a day, had a greater choice of subjects, and could combine school with home study as well as community-based classes. Although Freedom High had a waiting list, as a result of not being at school I got priority and soon found myself in a new educational world in which I flourished.

The plan at Freedom High was simple: the State of New Mexico had certain requirements for high school which involved, for example, a minimum of three years of English, two years of maths and science, and so on. You were assigned a mentor who would help you draw up your own personal study plan; you were free to study any subject anywhere and, in any way, you pleased, provided your plan met certain standards and fell in somewhere under the state-mandated graduation requirements. The mentor would then determine how much credit could be awarded for non-school-based classes and projects and met with you weekly to monitor your progress and help with any difficulties. Mentors also sometimes made home visits.

What a sense of empowerment! My personal experiences had led to my growing up quickly, and traditional American high school had no appeal. I felt ready for adult life and made up my mind to graduate as soon as possible. In the mornings I attended school classes on English, New Mexico State history, geometry and pottery; in the afternoons I wrote poetry and explored the meaning of life through personal study of world religions and philosophies, reading cover to cover through the Bible, Bhagavad Gita, Koran, Native American writings and other sacred texts. For PE, I learned Tai Chi and practiced yoga, and for Art I took private classes in jewellery-making. As an almost unheard-of privilege, I also attended first-year undergraduate courses in Environmental Physics and Introduction to Astronomy at the University of New Mexico, together with my father who had returned to university to complete his degree. We delighted in the other students' astonishment on hearing that we were father and daughter, thirty-six and fifteen years old; and we befriended the professor, a socialist who wore khaki trousers and white shirt every day of the year except May Day (when he wore red), and kept a private reserve of American bison at his home. Was it a suitably broad and rich educational experience? Absolutely, and I loved it.

My personal project was symbolic of the transition I was making to adulthood, during which time many teenagers need personal space. Not wanting to share a bedroom any longer with a younger sister and stepsister, I created my own bedroom in the far corner of our quarter acre of land: a hand-built Apache Wikiup partly dug out of the sandy soil, partly built of saplings and reeds that I collected from a nearby stream, following anthropologists' sketches. It was my retreat, my shelter and the cocoon from which I would emerge with new-found wings. And so, it was that on my sixteenth birthday the staff at Freedom High School decided that I had fulfilled the graduation requirements, two years earlier than usual, and was "as educated as any high school graduate they knew".

Although continuing complications in my personal life prevented me from enrolling immediately at university, the self-management and other important skills I learned during both my NYC primary education and my flexischooling experience at Freedom High contributed to my later confidence and success in education and at work.

Thirty-five years later, after obtaining my MA in Education and Advanced Diploma in Child Development and having experienced a variety of educational systems as both teacher and parent in the US, the Netherlands and the UK, I founded Manara Education CIC and the Manara Academy flexischooling programme in Leicester, partly in response to those inspiring early experiences at Freedom High School. Educational systems worldwide have become increasingly rigid and prescriptive over the past several decades, but governmental efforts to increase quality by increasing pressure on teachers and students have not yielded the desired results. In my view, the way to a better education for young people is not to create ever more detailed or stringent, soul-stifling targets, exams or inspection systems, but to allow children gradually to assume more responsibility for their own learning. That means starting with the child and respecting children and young people as the unique individuals that they are. This is not so much a matter of having faith in children per se, who are still immature, but in the innate potential and superb survival instincts of human beings, the most successful and adaptive creatures on earth. We seem to have forgotten that children are highly curious and are born asking "why?" and that they have an immense capacity to learn. Both research and experience show that given the opportunity and the right kind of environment and guidance, they will take the initiative to acquire the knowledge and skills they need to succeed in life.

At Manara Academy we are working on developing a model, based on the Montessori approach to primary education, that allows children to mature and pursue their own interests in developmentally appropriate ways while ensuring that they master the "three R's" and gain an adequate foundation for further studies. As we are a part-time school (at present twelve hours per week, but expanding to twenty as from September 2012), our children can enjoy the social benefits of being members of small, mixed-age classes as well as the benefits of home-education and community-based learning during non-school hours. Some of our parents enjoy spending more time and having a closer relationship with their children through home study and online courses, while others enrol their children in a wide variety of local classes and activities. All benefit from the personalised approach, and we have some early indications that they also make greater academic progress than they would in a traditional classroom setting.

We are in the early stages of establishing our school programme and culture, but have every hope that this model is a viable one for the future well-being of our children and society.

Fatima draws on her own personal educational experience particularly as a teenager at Freedom High School, Albuquerque, New Mexico, USA and is a testament to the efficacy of flexischooled education. Fatima was born in New York in 1960 and embraced Islam in 1979. She has an MA with Distinction in Education from Roehampton University and an Advanced Diploma in Child Development, is an author of several Muslim children's books and is pursuing a Montessori Primary Teacher qualification. She has been active in Islamic education for 20+ years in a variety of settings in the USA, Netherlands and UK including full-time and weekend Islamic schools, supplementary schools, Muslim Scouts and Girl Guides/Scouts. A founding Trustee of The Quest Foundation for Learning, Fatima has lifelong interest in holistic and Islamic education, spirituality, nature, and healthy, sustainable lifestyles.

Chapter 10. Campaign

Flexischooling is certainly enjoying a surge of interest which should be an indicator of real problems within the schooling system for a range of families and learners whose needs and aspirations are not being met.

The fundamental issue remains that the schooling system is so rigid, inertia ridden and bureaucratic that it is not sufficiently flexible and responsive to the needs of culture, society, families and learners.

Rather than looking to remove barriers, thereby increasing flexibility, efficiency and success, schooling seeks to maintain its narrow view of education. This rigidity is in itself problem for schooling... it places the system in an educational monoculture incapable of accepting and considering different points of view and transforming itself into a sustainable polyculture.

10.1 A Credible Option

Despite the fact that flexischooling is a lawful option there is an information vacuum within the system. Whether it's on entry to schooling, at the transitions, when major issues arise or at any other time it is not clear that flexischooling is something that families could consider and little advice and direction to enable it.

Further, it is highly unlikely that during the course of professional training or work that the majority of teachers would ever have come across the notion. The position remains that an effective lawful option remains hidden from families and educators.

Clearly, this information and our social media groups aim to help fill that void, but government and the DfE need to be a primary source of timely communication ensuring that flexischooling is known about widely and that can become an easily facilitated, credible option in a range of practical philosophical circumstances.

10.2 Alignment of Funding and Registration

Current funding, attendance and registration arrangements were not conceived with flexischooling in mind (and of course do not even consider the needs of any families educating otherwise with home education). This means that schools and local authorities see technical issues and problems rather than children, young people and learning. It makes the situation for schools, and particularly the decision-making head teachers unnecessarily problematic.

Flexischooling provides benefits for pupils, families, schools, communities and government. It offers something quite unique and special of which this country can and should be really proud.

The most obvious consideration is to look comprehensively at flexischooling and how it can be accommodated within the legal, funding, registration and guideline structures. This will necessitate a pause and consultation with those involved. Any review should look at flexischooling around the world, in Scotland (where it is part-time education / part-time home education and much simpler) as well as exploring how flexischooling could uniquely be used to support learners, families and the system to become more flexible, personalised and successful.

It would be advantageous to secure a universal understanding of the place and contributions of flexischooling to the educational landscape. Once established, the bureaucratic and administrative procedures and safeguards can be put in place and regular sensible review scheduled.

10.3 Campaigning

The Centre for Personalised Education is working on a range of fronts to campaign for flexischooling and support parents, learners and schools. It does this basically on the back of incredible commitment and expertise of its unpaid trustees and small group of volunteers. You can help advance the campaign by supporting us. See Chapter 11 for details of joining the Centre for Personalised Education. If you can offer any expertise or time you might like to join the Flexischooling Strategy Group. If so, contact Emma Dyke on the Flexischooling Families, UK Facebook forum.

10.4 Website

The Centre **for Personalised Education - website**[lxxix] has a comprehensive flexischooling section covering all aspects of the notion and providing up to date information briefing sheets for download.

10.5 Publications

Building on Prof Roland Meighan's initial publication Meighan, R. 1988, Flexischooling – education for tomorrow starting yesterday published under the

Education Now imprint (and still available at from Educational Heretics Press…we have published

- **PEN Journal 16. 2012 Flexischooling Special**[lxxx]
- **PEN Journal 17. 2012 Flexischooling Guidance Special**[lxxxi] **(updated version of J16)**
- This Flexischooling Handbook
- A broader flexischooling publication will be forthcoming.

10.6 Social Media

- **Centre for Personalised Education - website**[lxxxii]
- **CPE - Flexischooling Families UK -Facebook**[lxxxiii]
- **CPE - Flexischooling Practitioners UK - Facebook**[lxxxiv]
- **Centre for Personalised Education -Facebook**[lxxxv]
- **Home Education and your Local Authority: Help with dealing with officialdom**[lxxxvi]
- **Centre for Personalised Education -Personalised Education Now (Twitter)**[lxxxvii]
- **Centre for Personalised Education – Facebook Page**[lxxxviii]
- **Hollinsclough CE Primary Academy**[lxxxix]
- **Hollinsclough Flexischool Federation**[xc]
- **Educational Heretics Press - website**[xci]
- **Educational Heretics Press -Facebook Page**[xcii]
- **CPE - Light on Ed Research Network - Facebook**[xciii]
- **CPE - Legal Advice for Educational Startups - Facebook**[xciv]

10.7 Political Conversations

Wherever possible and within our capacity we actively

seek engagement with local authorities, the DfE and devolved administrations. We have links with politicians in both Houses. The Centre for Personalised Education stands ready to make the case for flexischooling within the political arena.

10.8 Small School Campaign

In 2018 we will be embarking in approaching all small schools under 100 pupils with information about the advantages of flexischooling. We will work with Hollinsclough in supporting schools with information and advice. If this goes well we will have established a critical mass of interest and can move on to all schools.

10.9 Learning Exchanges, Conferences and Local Events

We have run a series of learning exchanges (LEX) and conferences with flexischooling themes. We also support interested families with local events.

If you'd like to learn more and explore / encourage flexischooling in your area why don't you set up a local event on flexischooling? The Centre for Personalised Education Strategy Group will be happy to arrange speaker inputs if required and help you promote the event. Local events could be anything from 10 people upwards and conducted at any suitable venue where participants could cover the costs. Dates / days of week / times can be flexible and by arrangement.

Please get in touch with Emma Dyke using the Contact Us form[xcv]

Chapter 11. Media and Research

Media Contact - **Emma Dyke**[xcvi]

Research Contact - **Peter Humphreys**[xcvii]

11.1 In the Media

There's nothing irregular about flexi-schooling. Our rigid, semi-privatised British education system doesn't seem to like it, but part-time learning is great for kids. **Guardian Blog**[xcviii]

Flexing a School's Muscles. **Leadership Focus**[xcix]

More pupils at school with 'part time' scheme. **BBC Stoke**[c]

Flexischooling. **Head teacher Update** [ci]

Aged five and on flexi-time. **Guardian**[cii]

Best of both worlds: The new trend of flexi-schooling. **Independent.**[ciii]

The rise of flexi-schooling. With supersized primary schools, large class sizes and the squeeze on primary school places, some parents are choosing to educate their children at home for part of the week. **Guardian.**[civ]

'Flexitime' school that rewrites the book on teaching. **Independent.** [cv]

Hollinsclough CE Primary Academy. There are a range of links regarding flexischooling and the media on the school's **Flexischooling page**[cvi]

11.2 Research

Meighan, R. (1988)'Flexischooling. Education for tomorrow, starting yesterday'. Education Now, Ticknall

Gutherson, P. and Mountford-Lees, J. (2010) **New models for organising education: Flexi schooling - how one school does it well:**[cvii] CfBT Education Trust

Dr Clare Lawrence – Writing and research on flexischooling and autism. **Clare Lawrence Website.**[cviii]

Janette Mountford Lees, Head teacher at Hollinsclough completed a piece of research with a Farmington Fellowship (Oxford University) in 2014 Flexischooling – A Matter of Choice again based upon the Hollinsclough experience.

Currently there are a number of researchers who are or will be researching flexischooling with Hollinsclough CE Primary School. There is also some research being commissioned by **The parents Science Gang**[cix] in Scotland.

Lynda O'Sullivan, one of the Hollinsclough staff has done her own research project on the effectiveness and impact of flexischooling at the school.

11.3 References

This volume –

Humphreys, P. (2018) A Guide to Flexischooling in England and Wales. (E-Book. Kindle edition) Centre for Personalised Education / Educational Heretics Press, Walsall / Shrewsbury, England.

Black, J. (2017) The Power of One Becoming the Power

139

of Many. Personalised Education Now Journal 26. Special.), Centre for Personalised Education, Walsall, England.

Humphreys, P. (2017) Neoliberal Schooling, Dehumanisation and an Education in Rudd, T. & Goodson, I. F. [Eds.] (2017). Negotiating Neoliberalism: Developing Alternative Educational Visions. Sense Publishers. Rotterdam/Boston/Taipei[cx].

Mayfield, R. (2107) Flexischooling – What it is, Why it works and What to do at Home. ISBN-13:978-1-5440-0355-9 Self Published Volume accessed from Amazon

Mountford-Lees, J. (2104) Flexischooling - A Matter of Choice. Farmington Fellowship, (Published in MS PowerPoint) Oxford University, Oxford.

Humphreys, P. (2014d) Rethinking Learning and Lives 2040: Educational Technologies and Personalised Learning Landscapes. Journal of Personalised Education Now. No.21. Nottingham.

Humphreys, P. (2014c) Rethinking Learning and Lives 2040: Educational Technologies and Personalised Learning Landscapes. Resisting Neoliberal Education Project. University of Brighton.

Humphreys, P. (2014b) Life and work of Roland Meighan. Journal of Personalised Education Now. No.20. Nottingham.

Humphreys, P. (2014a) Educational Technologies and Personalised Learning Landscapes 2040. Web-based article in Rethinking Educational Technology Scenarios. Resisting Neoliberal Education Project. University of Brighton.

Lawrence, C. (2012) Autism and Flexischooling: A Shared Classroom and Homeschooling Approach. Jessica Kingsley, London

Personalised Education Now (2012) Personalised Education Now Journal 17. Special. Flexischooling Guidance)[cxi], Centre for Personalised Education, Nottingham.

Gutherson, P. and Mountford-Lees, J. (2010) New models for organising education: Flexi schooling - how one school does it well:[cxii] CfBT Education Trust

Meighan, R. (2004) Comparing Learning Systems, the Good, the Bad, the Ugly and the Counterproductive, Educational Heretics Press, Nottingham

Meighan, R. (1988) 'Flexischooling. Education for tomorrow, starting yesterday'. Education Now, Ticknall

Chapter 12. Support the Centre for Personalised Education

The Centre for Personalised Education has a long and illustrious history the evolution the organisation is based on the stunning productivity of such a small group of passionate educators.

Timeline:

Education Now Publishing Co-op 1988-2004
- 16 years
- 64 News and Review Magazines
- 40 Special Supplements
- Some 20 Education Now books

Education Unlimited Consultancy 1994-1996
- 2 years – consultancy and mentoring activity

Institute for Democracy 1994-1997?
- 3 years
- 3 conferences

Educational Heretics Press 1988-2008
- 21 years
- 80+ books

Centre for Personalised Education 1995- Present
- 26 journals
- 50 conferences / Learning Exchanges (LEX)
- Website
- Social Media support groups / networks

Membership of the Centre for Personalised Education

The Centre for Personalised Education welcomes members, both individuals and groups, who support and promote its vision.

Its membership includes educators in learning centres, home educating settings, schools, colleges and universities. Members range across interested individuals and families, teachers, head teachers, advisers, inspectors and academics. **The Centre for Personalised Education** has extensive national and international links.

Above all the issues of personalised education and learning are issues with relevance to every man, woman and child because they lie at the heart of what kind of society we wish to live in.

Membership Includes:

- Two **CPE-PEN** journals a year (choice of hard copy or digital)
- Annual Learning Exchange(s) (usually free to members)
- Conferences (usually free to members)
- The support of a diverse network of learners and educators in the field of personalised education. Free advice and signposting.
- Ongoing research and publications in collaboration with various projects, settings and Educational Heretics Press[cxiii]
- Regular E-Newsletters to membership

- Access to interest and support groups and forums.
- Centre for Personalised Education - website[cxiv]
- CPE - Flexischooling Families UK -Facebook[cxv]
- CPE - Flexischooling Practitioners UK -Facebook[cxvi]
- Centre for Personalised Education -Facebook[cxvii]
- Home Education and your Local Authority: Help with dealing with officialdom[cxviii]
- Centre for Personalised Education -Personalised Education Now (Twitter)[cxix]
- Centre for Personalised Education – Facebook Page[cxx]
- CPE - Light on Ed Research Network - Facebook[cxxi]
- CPE - Legal Advice for Educational Startups - Facebook[cxxii]

The membership subscription is £25 per year (£12 unwaged)

Please print off the Membership Form[cxxiii] and return

About Educational Heretics press

Founded in 1984 by Dr Roland Meighan and Janet Meighan, EHP also handles orders for Education Now publishing Cooperative (founded 1970).

EHP has published approximately 90 titles aiming to challenge educational dogma with particular emphasis on personalised learning and home education, putting the learner at the centre of the process.

EHP is now run by Mike Wood. Our website (where further titles can be purchased) is:

www.educationalhereticspress.com

Bibliography - Digital Links

i www.educationalhereticspress.com/

ii www.personalisededucationnow.org.uk/

iii www.personalisededucationnow.org.uk/

iv www.facebook.com/groups/380046592033979/

v www.facebook.com/groups/133020056831365/

vi www.facebook.com/groups/1607166472854561/

vii www.facebook.com/groups/239232119524989/

viii @cpe_pen

ix www.facebook.com/personalisededucationnow/

x hollinsclough.staffs.sch.uk/

xi www.flexischoolfederation.co.uk/

xii www.educationalhereticspress.com/

xiii www.facebook.com/educationalhereticspress/

xiv www.facebook.com/groups/767234383469198/

xv www.facebook.com/groups/1952907924769214/

xvi www.personalisededucationnow.org.uk/law-and-guidance/

xvii www.gov.uk/government/publications/school-admissions-code--2

xviii www.personalisededucationnow.org.uk/concept/part-time-attendance-england-dec-16/

xix www.personalisededucationnow.org.uk/law-and-guidance/

xx www.gov.uk/government/uploads/system/uploads/attachment_data/file/288135/guidelines_for_las_on_elective_home_educationsecondrevisev2_0.pdf

xxi www.personalisededucationnow.org.uk/law-and-guidance/is-flexischooling-legal-in-england-v1-april-17/

xxii www.personalisededucationnow.org.uk/parent-info/parents-leaflet-v1-feb-17-1/

xxiii www.personalisededucationnow.org.uk/concept/part-time-attendance-england-dec-16/

xxiv www.gov.uk/government/uploads/system/uploads/

attachment_data/file/389388/School_Admissions_
Code_2014_-_19_Dec.pdf

[xxv] www.personalisededucationnow.org.uk/concept/

[xxvi] www.personalisededucationnow.org.uk/pen-journals/

[xxvii] www.flexischoolfederation.co.uk/

[xxviii] hollinsclough.staffs.sch.uk/Flexi.htm

[xxix] www.personalisededucationnow.org.uk/pen-journals/

[xxx] hollinsclough.staffs.sch.uk/Flexi.htm

[xxxi] www.personalisededucationnow.org.uk/finding-flexi-positive-schools/parents-negotiating-with-schools-leaflet-july-12th-2017/

[xxxii] www.personalisededucationnow.org.uk/flexischooling-info-sheets/

[xxxiii] www.gov.uk/government/publications/school-admissions-code--2

[xxxiv] www.gov.uk/government/publications/school-admissions-code--2

[xxxv] www.personalisededucationnow.org.uk/law-and-guidance/is-flexischooling-legal-in-england-v1-april-17/

[xxxvi] www.personalisededucationnow.org.uk/school-info/head-teacher-leaflet-v3-may-17/

[xxxvii] www.personalisededucationnow.org.uk/concept/

[xxxviii] www.personalisededucationnow.org.uk/concept/

[xxxix] www.personalisededucationnow.org.uk/contracts/

[xl] www.personalisededucationnow.org.uk/

[xli] www.facebook.com/groups/380046592033979/

[xlii] www.facebook.com/groups/133020056831365/

[xliii] www.facebook.com/groups/1607166472854561/

[xliv] www.facebook.com/groups/239232119524989/

[xlv] @cpe_pen

[xlvi] www.facebook.com/personalisededucationnow/

[xlvii] hollinsclough.staffs.sch.uk/

[xlviii] www.flexischoolfederation.co.uk/

[xlix] www.educationalhereticspress.com/

147

i www.facebook.com/educationalhereticspress/

ii www.facebook.com/groups/767234383469198/

iii www.facebook.com/groups/1952907924769214/

iiii www.personalisededucationnow.org.uk/school-info/head-teacher-leaflet-v3-may-17/

liv www.personalisededucationnow.org.uk/law-and-guidance/is-flexischooling-legal-in-england-v1-april-17/

lv www.personalisededucationnow.org.uk/law-and-guidance/is-flexischooling-legal-in-england-v1-april-17/

lvi hollinsclough.staffs.sch.uk/Flexi.htm

lvii www.personalisededucationnow.org.uk/law-and-guidance/is-flexischooling-legal-in-england-v1-april-17/

lviii www.gov.uk/government/publications/school-attendance.

lix www.flexischoolfederation.co.uk/

lx www.facebook.com/groups/133020056831365/

lxi www.personalisededucationnow.org.uk/pen-journals/

lxii www.flexischoolfederation.co.uk/

lxiii www.clarelawrenceautism.com/

lxiv www.personalisededucationnow.org.uk/minischooling/

lxv www.hollinsclough.staffs.sch.uk/Flexi.htm

lxvi www.erpinghamprimaryschool.co.uk/

lxvii www.college.selfmanagedlearning.org/

lxviii tinyurl.com/7u28k3u

lxix www.personalisededucationnow.org.uk/pen-journals/

lxx www.jkp.com/uk/autism-and-flexischooling.html

lxxi hollinsclough.staffs.sch.uk/

lxxii www.erpinghamprimaryschool.co.uk/smartweb/school/flexi-schooling

lxxiii www.personalisededucationnow.org.uk/pen-journals/

lxxiv www.eddistutorial.com/

lxxv www.personalisededucationnow.org.uk/pen-journals/

lxxvi www.interhigh.co.uk/

lxxvii www.funtech.co.uk/

lxxviii www.personalisededucationnow.org.uk/pen-journals/

[lxxix] www.personalisededucationnow.org.uk/

[lxxx] ed_now_1997_newsreview_16/

[lxxxi] www.personalisededucationnow.org.uk/wp-content/uploads/2016/02/PEN-Journal17.-2012-FLEXISCHOOLING-GUIDANCE-SPECIAL.doc

[lxxxii] www.personalisededucationnow.org.uk/

[lxxxiii] www.facebook.com/groups/380046592033979/

[lxxxiv] www.facebook.com/groups/133020056831365/

[lxxxv] www.facebook.com/groups/1607166472854561/

[lxxxvi] www.facebook.com/groups/239232119524989/

[lxxxvii] @cpe_pen

[lxxxviii] www.facebook.com/personalisededucationnow/

[lxxxix] hollinsclough.staffs.sch.uk/

[xc] www.flexischoolfederation.co.uk/

[xci] www.educationalhereticspress.com/

[xcii] www.facebook.com/educationalhereticspress/

[xciii] www.facebook.com/groups/767234383469198/

[xciv] www.facebook.com/groups/1952907924769214/

[xcv] www.personalisededucationnow.org.uk/contact-us/

[xcvi] www.personalisededucationnow.org.uk/contact-us/

[xcvii] www.personalisededucationnow.org.uk/contact-us/

[xcviii] www.theguardian.com/theobserver/she-said/2014/sep/25/theres-nothing-irregular-about-flexi-schooling

[xcix] www.hollinsclough.staffs.sch.uk\Flexi files\Leadership Focus Oct 2011.pdf

[c] www.bbc.co.uk/news/uk-england-stoke-staffordshire-12173283

[ci] www.headteacher-update.com\cgi-bin\go.pl\article\article.html?uid=83899;type_uid=79;section=Features

[cii] www.guardian.co.uk\education\2009\jun\23\home-schooling-early-years-education

[ciii] www.independent.co.uk/news/education/schools/best-of-both-worlds-the-new-trend-of-flexischooling-1976414.html

[civ] www.guardian.co.uk/education/2011/dec/05/rise-of-flexi-

schooling

[cv] www.independent.co.uk/news/education/education-news/flexitime-school-that-rewrites-the-book-on-teaching-2298708.html

[cvi] hollinsclough.staffs.sch.uk/Flexi.htm

[cvii] www.cfbt.com/evidenceforeducation/our_research/evidence_for_government/alternative_education/flexi_schooling.aspx

[cviii] www.clarelawrenceautism.com/

[cix] parentingsciencegang.org.uk/web-chats/the-great-flexischooling-survey/

[cx] www.sensepublishers.com/catalogs/bookseries/studies-in-professional-life-and-work/negotiating-neoliberalism/

[cxi] www.personalisededucationnow.org.uk/pen-journals/

[cxii] www.cfbt.com/evidenceforeducation/our_research/evidence_for_government/alternative_education/flexi_schooling.aspx

[cxiii] www.educationalhereticspress.com/

[cxiv] www.personalisededucationnow.org.uk/

[cxv] www.facebook.com/groups/380046592033979/

[cxvi] www.facebook.com/groups/133020056831365/

[cxvii] www.facebook.com/groups/1607166472854561/

[cxviii] www.facebook.com/groups/239232119524989/

[cxix] @cpe_pen

[cxx] www.facebook.com/personalisededucationnow/

[cxxi] www.facebook.com/groups/767234383469198/

[cxxii] www.facebook.com/groups/1952907924769214/

[cxxiii] www.personalisededucationnow.org.uk/join-us-membership/membership-form-renewal-form-2018-2019/

Printed in Great Britain
by Amazon

36109856R00085